C000155654

DOWN IN MY HEART TO STAY

EXPERIENCING GOD'S JOY

COMPILED BY HAYES PRESS

Down In My Heart To Stay: Experiencing God's Joy

Copyright © 2015 by Hayes Press

All rights reserved. Printed in the United Kingdom. No part of this book may be used or reproduced in any manner whatsoever without written permission except in the case of brief quotations embodied in critical articles or reviews.

Unless otherwise indicated, all Scripture quotations are from are from the Holy Bible, New International Version®, NIV® Copyright © 1973, 1978, 1984, 2011 by Biblica, Inc.™ Used by permission. All rights reserved. Scriptures marked NKJV are from the New King James Version® (NKJV®). Copyright © 1982 Thomas Nelson, Inc. Used by permission. All rights reserved worldwide. Scriptures marked NASB are from the New American Standard Bible®, Copyright © 1960, 1962, 1963, 1968, 1971, 1972, 1973, 1975, 1977, 1995 by The Lockman Foundation Used by permission. (www.Lockman.org)

Published by Hayes Press (**www.hayespress.org**)

The Barn, Flaxlands, Royal Wootton Bassett, Wiltshire, UK SN4 8DY 01793 850598

Book and Cover design by Hayden Press. For information contact: haydenpress2011@gmail.com

If you enjoy reading this book, please consider taking a moment to leave a positive review on Amazon.

ISBN: 9781871126242

First Edition: September 2015

10 9 8 7 6 5 4 3 2 1

CONTENTS

1: WANING JOY

J oy can be such an elusive thing, yet why should it be? Why should the child of God feel that Christian living is just something to be coped with, a struggle, a warfare without victory, resulting in true joy being a remote possibility rather than a living reality? Where can we learn the secret that will overcome this spirit of defeatism and allow a lasting sense of joy to accompany the believer? Go back to the Upper Room. Listen to the Master as He speaks with His disciples: "I have told you this so that my joy may be in you and that your joy may be complete. Greater love has no one than this: to lay down one's life for one's friends." (John 15:11,13)

Listen, again, as He speaks to His Father. "Father, the hour has come ... I am coming to You now; but I say these things while I am still in the world, so that they may have the full measure of My joy within them" (John 17:1,13). Isn't the lesson here? In the very anticipation of Calvary, the Saviour has thoughts of joy and is pleased to share them with His friends, His Father and, through the divine record, with us. His joy is related to the sacrifice of Himself and to what is to be accomplished through His death. Consequently we look off unto Him, "Who for the joy set before Him ... endured the cross" (Hebrews 12:2).

And so, we learn that in the ways of God joy is bound up inseparably with sacrifice. This was made clear in Exodus 29:38-42 where God set out His daily requirement. The offering of two lambs, one in the morning and one in the evening, was the great foreshadowing of Christ in death God's Lamb. He was crucified in the morning (the third hour - Mark 15:25) and yielded Himself to God in the evening (the ninth hour - Mark 15:34). With each lamb a drink-offering was to be brought, for God could not see Calvary's sacrifice without Calvary's joy. For this reason the fourth part of an hin of wine was to be poured out on each lamb "Wine which cheers both God and man" (Judges 9:13 NKJV).

But how could wine cheer God? In Jotham's parable of the trees the vine probably referred to the drink-offering. Exodus 29 is God's commandment to His priests. Numbers 15 is His commandment to His people. In the latter, He spoke in anticipation of the people entering the land. Was not their joy to be manifestly full in the place of fullness? Was this where their joy was to be seen in accompaniment with their offerings? Without doubt, God had little pleasure from His people in the wilderness. Through disobedience they journeyed there for forty years, having failed to submit their will to the will of God. To cross Jordan was to enter the place where the divine will was in control, where victories through faith were assured and where their joy would be displayed. What an experience: to walk in fullest agreement with Him and, through the submission of the will, know increasing joy!

Note the progression in Numbers 15 - the fourth part of an hin, the third part of an hin, and half an hin. Increasing joy! Perhaps you look back on earlier days in your life and feel that joy has decreased. Is it that yours is a waning joy? In a certain sense, has the half become a third and then a quarter? Has something interrupted your communion with the Lord, and now you seek the way to fulness? Nevertheless, even if waning joy has resulted from waning communion, God speaks once, yea twice. He spoke to Jacob in Genesis 31:13: "Now leave this land at once ..." He spoke again in chapter 35:1: "Go up to Bethel, and settle there..."

What a disservice we do ourselves when God's "now" becomes our "later"! Consciously or otherwise it is the glorification of the self-will. It's tragic when we imply by our actions that we know better than He does. However, Jacob and his household went, returning at the entreaties of God and, on arrival, set up a pillar and poured out a drink-offering. Glad to be back, what joy! But before they went back they had to rid themselves of certain things. Note them carefully as they put away their strange gods, purify themselves and change their garments. In the pursuit of holiness we must learn, as they did, that the way back cannot be travelled with the things that kept us back. Idols, uncleanness, and an acknowledged poor testimony must be overcome in every generation.

As God calls us to face up to these things, it may be that joy is being withheld because we withhold ourselves and allow lesser things to occupy our time and attention. Such things come between ourselves and God. And that is idolatry!

There are some things in our lives that would be better buried, never to rise to disturb our walk again. Jacob hid the idols, buried beneath the oak. How much we lose if we fail to enter into an experimental understanding of Galatians 6:14: "May I never boast except in the cross of our Lord Jesus Christ, through which the world has been crucified to me, and I to the world". Beneath that tree we are able to leave our idols! The pouring out of the drink-offering at Bethel was ample proof of Jacob's unhindered joy and a lesson to us that...

Waning joy can be the result of waning commitment
In Joel's day God was greatly dissatisfied. The sad commentary is set out in the first chapter of his prophecy.

Verse 9: The drink-offering is cut off from the house of the LORD.
Verse 10: The new wine is dried up (Hebrew: withered).

Verse 12: The vine is withered, joy is withered away from the sons of men.

Verse 16: Is not the meat cut off before our eyes, yea, joy and gladness from the house of our God?

How striking the relationship among the vine, drink-offering and joy in these verses: cut off, withered. Absolute barrenness! The land, the people and the house of God each bore the mark of it. Of course, if there is no gleaning there can be no giving, and if there is no giving there can be no gladness. The only remedy would be a complete turning to God. The rending of the heart must precede the blessing of the Lord. Deep, heartfelt, out-poured confession must precede the restoration of the drink-offering, (Joel 2:12-14) from the hand of a gracious God who ever waits to bless the contrite. Unless we know what it is to be broken before Him we will miss His clear indication that ...

Waning joy can be the result of waning confession

Perhaps, as we look at the various presentations of the drink-offering, we wonder: Wherein lies the challenge for ourselves? If we truly desire to know it, the Holy Spirit will direct our thoughts as He did the apostle Paul's. He spoke of pouring himself out as a drink-offering "upon the sacrifice and service" of the faith of the saints in Philippi. He was not only prepared to do it, but confessed "I rejoice and share my joy with you all" (Philippians 2:17 NASB).

What a Christ-centred ministry: ready to pour himself out as an imitator of his Saviour, even unto death (2 Timothy 4:6)! Why pour out? Why seek joy at such a cost? For how much it had cost Paul to be such a sentinel of divine truth. No doubt he would join with Peter in saying, "but rejoice to the extent that you partake of Christ's sufferings, that when His glory is revealed, you may also be glad with exceeding joy" (1 Peter 4:13 NKJV).

The secret of joy was in the surrendered life, then and now. If we share Paul's enjoyment of the Saviour and his all-absorbing hunger - "that I may gain Christ" - we have learned the secret. But we will only gain Him to the degree that we allow Him to gain us! God only gathers up what we pour out.

How much God received from Hannah! What a fullness she possessed as she made her way to Shiloh! Some would have noted the value of her offering of three bullocks. It was so much to give, but God saw more than that. He saw her ephah of fine flour for the meal-offering. Had He asked her for that? No. All she was due to take was three tenths of an ephah for each animal, but overflowing joy could never stop at nine tenths. She had to give ten tenths. Joy had conquered duty! The more perceptive onlooker would have seen her skin of wine and grasped the significant fact that she was going up with joy. Her silence was turned to audible praise, her sorrow to joy and yet, at the heart of her experience was sacrifice, giving up her boy for the service of God.

Years later another mother came, not with the riches of Hannah but claiming God's provision for the poor. With her Son she took two turtle doves, the sign of her poverty. But richer than Hannah she is, for hers is not the bringing of Samuel to God, but the bringing of Immanuel. Where was the expression of her joy? Had she no wine? No drink-offering? It was not hers to give. He would give it Himself. In that Upper Room He took the cup of wine and poured it out, the emblem of His precious blood poured out for us. He delighted to do the will of His Father and poured Himself out as the true Drink-offering. What giving and what joy!

The Lord Himself and none beside
Its bitterness could know,
Nor other tell the joy's full tide
That from that cup shall flow.

The secret of our joy will be in the sacrifice of ourselves. In the satisfying of Him there will be the satisfying of ourselves. A life of communion, commitment and confession is the route we must all travel. A consuming passion for the Saviour, a pre-occupation with the will of God and a Spirit-filled addiction to the field of service must occupy our undivided attention. If so engaged, we will learn the reality of true discipleship. Is it not only in this that, sacrificially, we will overcome the waning joy? Now, not later!

2: THE JOY OF THE LORD

The story has been told of a man who arrived in Liverpool where he was to embark for his journey to America. As he had very little money, he decided to economise on food during the voyage, and bought himself some crackers and cheese from a small shop. As the voyage progressed, the sea air made him very hungry, as well as making his crackers soft; and to make matters worse, he caught a whiff of some food on a tray which was being carried by a steward. He was unable to hold out any longer, and although short of money, he asked the steward the price of a good meal in the ship's restaurant. Imagine his amazement when he found that all his meals were included in the price of the ticket for the voyage: he could have eaten as much as he wanted!

It seems that many people put their trust in the Lord Jesus Christ and accept Him as their Saviour, but never really appropriate the blessings which are theirs for the taking. The joy of the Lord is not restricted in any way, but is a Christian grace to be appropriated by all, to be shared with, and shown to others. It is sad that unbelievers often associate the Christian gospel with joylessness and a mournful demeanour. One man was offering tracts to passers-by, and, in a mournful tone, asked a man if he would like to be a Christian. "No thank you", replied the man, "I've enough troubles of my own". We could have told him that "the cheerful heart has a continual feast"

(Proverbs 15:15); and that "The kingdom of God is ... righteousness and peace and joy in the Holy Spirit" (Romans 14:17).

Joy in Believing

It is necessary, sometimes, to distinguish between joy and happiness. It has been said that "happiness depends on what happens", but joy is independent of circumstances. It is possible to have a sort of superficial happiness, as is witnessed by multitudes of non-Christians, but joy clearly emanates from God Himself. This is a fact recognized by Old Testament writers, as well as those who wrote the New. "The joy of the LORD is your strength", Nehemiah told the people of Israel at a time of repentance arising from the reading of the Word of God (Nehemiah 8:10). "The God of hope fill you with all JOY and peace as you trust him", wrote Paul to the church in Rome (Romans 15:13).

The unique quality of the joy of the Lord is recognized when it is appreciated that it is the same joy which the Lord Jesus Christ possessed, and indeed passed on to His disciples: "I have told you this so that my joy may be in you and that your joy may be complete" (John 15:11). Who can describe the joy which comes to the soul when an earnest seeker first puts his or her trust in the Lord! Many of God's children will continue to testify of the peace which has remained with them: perhaps not as many can still speak of the joy which they experienced in that first moment of release from the powers of darkness.

Joy in Service

The service of God was never meant to be a dreary or a mournful duty. It should always be expressive of the joy in the heart of the worshipper or worker. It is said of the disciples, following their meeting with the risen Lord: "They worshipped Him, and returned to Jerusalem with great joy: and were continually in the temple, blessing God" (Luke 24:52). David gave some indication of the divine joy when he said, "you will fill me with joy in your presence, with eternal pleasures at your right hand." (Psalm 16:11). It is David, perhaps, who puts so many words of joy into our hearts, (and on our lips!), in our worship of the same God in whom he trusted, when we capture some of the sheer exuberance which was his, and break forth into praise: "I will bless the LORD at all times: His praise shall continually be in my mouth ... O magnify the LORD with me, and let us exalt His name together" (Psalm 34:1,3).

In the service of stewardship, Paul wrote concerning the churches in Macedonia: "In the midst of a very severe trial, their overflowing joy and their extreme poverty welled up in rich generosity" (2 Corinthians 8:2). The possibility of the final sacrifice in service was never very far from Paul, but this never caused him to be in any way despondent. He wrote when faced with such possibility, "I am glad and rejoice with all of you. So you too should be glad and rejoice with me" (Philippians 2:17,18).

Joy in Affliction
It is the prophet Habakkuk who perhaps makes affliction all seem like nothing when he says in his psalm:

"For though the fig tree shall not blossom,
Neither shall fruit be in the vines;
The labour of the olive shall fail,
And the fields shall yield no meat;
The flock shall be cut off from the fold,
And there shall be no herd in the stalls;
Yet I will rejoice in the LORD,
I will joy in the God of my salvation" (Habbakuk 3:17-18).

The joy of the Lord was truly his strength! "Sorrowful, yet always rejoicing", said the apostle Paul in 2 Corinthians 6:10; and again, "I am greatly encouraged; in all our troubles my joy knows no bounds." (2 Corinthians 7:4). It was not just a case of having sufficient joy for his own comfort when passing through great trial, but he spoke of actually "overflowing with joy" when pressed on every side. What a great character was Paul! And old James seemed to be in the same mind when he wrote, "Consider it pure joy, my brothers and sisters, whenever you face trials of many kinds, [3]because you know that the testing of your faith produces perseverance" (James 1:2-3). And then there was Peter, that great strengthener of his brothers, when he wrote with particular reference to persecution, "But rejoice inasmuch as you participate in the sufferings of Christ, so that you may be overjoyed when his glory is revealed" (1 Peter 4:13). Afflictions, persecution and trials are to be regarded as additional causes for joyfulness: a peculiar and quite remarkable witness to the unbeliever.

Joy in Witness

It must be fairly clear from a number of the scriptures already quoted that the joy of the Lord is not something that can be bottled up. The peace that we have in the Lord Jesus Christ will probably be noticed by others in our serenity in the face of trouble, in our unruffled behaviour in the face of external pressures, and in our refusal to get over-anxious in matters over which we have not the least bit of control.

Some Christians seem to find it necessary to demonstrate their joy in a noisy kind of way. A reverent use of the expression "Praise the Lord" may be acceptable, but a great deal of shouting and jumping up and down may give the appearance of carnality. So how is our joy observed by others? There is no doubt that the joy of the Lord puts a melody into the heart, and causes the voice to sing, hence Paul's exhortation: "Be filled with the Spirit; speaking one to another in psalms and hymns and spiritual songs, singing and making melody with your heart to the Lord" (Ephesians 5:18-20).

The prophet Isaiah found it hard to contain himself, for he wrote, "I delight greatly in the LORD; my soul rejoices in my God. For he has clothed me with garments of salvation and arrayed me in a robe of his righteousness, as a bridegroom adorns his head like a priest, and as a bride adorns herself with her jewels. For as the soil makes the sprout come up and a garden causes seeds to grow, so the Sovereign LORD will make righteousness and praise spring up before all nations" (Isaiah 61:10,11). The most natural outcome of joy in the soul must be praise in the heart and praise on the lips. How else could Paul and Silas have responded other than by joyful praise when they prayed and sang hymns to God at midnight bound fast in jail? The witness of the individual, and the witness of the church, will be all the more vital when both are seen to be unrestrained in their praise.

"The fruit of the Spirit is ... joy" (Galatians 5:22). Spirit-filled hearts, surrendered lives, may be assured of a joy which the world can never know, because of their attachment to the Lord Jesus Himself: "Though you have not seen him, you love him; and even though you do not see him now, you believe in him and are filled with an inexpressible and glorious joy" (1 Peter 1:8). Believing and rejoicing hearts will always find yet greater joy in the anticipation of the return of their Lord, and His own words to His disciples will always come over loud and clear: "I will see you again and you will rejoice, and no one will take away your joy" (John 16:22). Can anyone ask for more? "Rejoice in the Lord always. I will say it again: Rejoice!" (Philippians 4:4).

3: THE JOY OF THE KINGDOM

For the kingdom of God is not a matter of eating and drinking, but of righteousness, peace and joy in the Holy Spirit, because anyone who serves Christ in this way is pleasing to God and receives human approval." (Romans 14:17,18).

The kingdom of God is the rule of God among the people of God. When the word of God is willingly obeyed, then there is righteousness and peace and joy in the Holy Spirit. This kingdom cannot be seen or entered apart from the new birth (John 3:3-5). The unrighteous cannot inherit the kingdom of God (1 Corinthians 6:9-10). No thieves or covetous persons; no drunkards or revilers; no fornicators or idolaters have part in it.

What conditions should prevail in the kingdom? Righteousness and peace and joy in the Holy Spirit! If any one of these is lacking, then it is time for us to have a searching of heart. Let us not pretend to be, what we really are not. We do not commend the truth of God if we are joyless, or sharp, or critical, or unkind, however correct we may be in doctrine. Let us not be content with a position in the kingdom, if the characteristics of the kingdom are not found in our lives.

Righteousness and peace! These are inseparable companions. This poor sin-sick world has tried hard, from the beginning of time, to separate them. They want to have peace without righteousness, but this cannot be. They cannot be separated, for God has joined them together. They are the heritage of all who obey the Lord. Peace is the worthy companion of righteousness, always and everywhere

Joy completes this delightful trio, the joy of the Lord. In the hearts of all who love the Lord, and who love His saints, there is joy. How much we need to guard against anything that would rob us of it, for the joy of the Lord is our strength (Nehemiah 8:10). Little faith will rob us of it. Let us count upon the faithfulness of God, and our own faith and joy will grow exceedingly. Let us love one another from the heart fervently, and then all unwise criticism and harsh speaking will cease, and peace and joy will fill our hearts.

When the remnant of Judah returned to Jerusalem, we read that "the joy of Jerusalem was heard afar off" (Nehemiah 12:43). What great days those were! Paul wrote in his captivity "Rejoice in the Lord always: again I will say, Rejoice". If joy is lacking in our spiritual service, then let us search our hearts for the cause. Let us not be satisfied with the positional expression of the kingdom of God, valuable though that is. Let the joy of the people of God be heard in every assembly, and then it will be noised abroad. We have nothing to learn about joy from this poor distressed world. Let our joy in the Lord be manifest to those around us, and many who see and hear will seek deliverance from the toils of sin, and will be drawn to Him who has put a new song into our mouths.

"Worship the LORD with gladness; come before him with joyful songs. Know that the LORD is God. It is he who made us, and we are his; we are his people, the sheep of his pasture. Enter his gates with thanksgiving and his courts with praise; give thanks to him and praise his name. (Psalm 100:2-4).

4: THE RIVER OF DELIGHTS

I t's inherent in the human race to seek after happiness. Generation after generation seeks it in numerous ways, each trying by its own methods to be happier than the last. All these efforts they enjoy fleetingly (Hebrews 11:25).

God's desire is that His people should be happy! In His word He has revealed ways and means by which we can know real, deep, lasting pleasure. Unlike the joy of men, it is not dependent upon men's devices. So there is no stagnation, it is always clear and fresh, and is like the river of which we read, "You give them drink from you river of delights" (Psalm 36:8). We would, however, remind ourselves that certain conditions are attached to this promise in Psalm 36:

(1) taking refuge under "the shadow of Your wings"
(2) being abundantly satisfied with "the abundance of Your house."

These two requirements form part of the pleasure that God desires all should enjoy. Let us view this river at its source, then note its gradual expansion. It must be borne in mind that the pleasure of God is found in Christ and the things of Christ, for "the pleasure of the LORD shall prosper in His hand" (Isaiah 53:10). We have all known, we trust, the deep, soul-stirring joy of salvation. Laden with our guilt, and on our way to hell, we came to Christ, "who His own self bear our sins in His body upon the tree". By faith we saw the One who was "wounded for our transgressions". It was then that the burden of our hearts rolled away. In this God would have us to be happy, and that our joy should be constant, knowing no fluctuation. So it is written, "Blessed (happy) are those whose transgressions are forgiven, whose sins are covered. Blessed (happy) is the one whose sin the LORD will never count against them" (Psalm 32:1,2; Romans 4:6-8).

The apostle Peter strikes a joyful note when he says, "Though you have not seen him, you love him; and even though you do not see him now, you believe in him and are filled with an inexpressible and glorious joy" (1 Peter 1:8). Here we drank for the first time of the river of His pleasures. Here we were filled with a great joy, an unspeakable joy, and we went on our way rejoicing.

Sometimes our joy is disturbed. Unwittingly, it may be, we are overcome by some sin, or by something the devil is using to mar our happiness in Christ. David was brought low because of sin which overwhelmed him, and his joy fled. But what heart-searchings were his, what confession, what crying unto God for mercy, for washing, for cleansing! Notice his plea, "Restore to me the joy of Your salvation" (Psalm 51:12).

When Paul preached the gospel to the Galatians, they received it, and the messenger, with joy, so that he wrote "you welcomed me as if I were an angel of God, as if I were Christ Jesus himself" (Galatians 4:14). Later he was perplexed over them, and seemed to have become their enemy, why? Because Satan had insinuated into their hearts that which marred the purity and simplicity of the gospel which Paul had preached. They had been deluded into accepting spurious teaching which brought them into bondage. Remembering their former experience, he writes "Where then is your blessing of me now?" (Galatians 4:15). Where was that happiness of theirs? How he longed that there might be with them a restoring of the joy of their salvation! May we ever keep near the cross, the fountain of our gladness!

Our faith should expand, and a constant trust in God should be manifested in our lives. Day by day our confidence in Him should develop. We have known His blessing in salvation, now we should look for His constant providential care. "Trust in the LORD with all your heart, and lean not on your own understanding. In all your ways submit to Him, and He will make your paths straight" (Proverbs 3:5,6).

"Trust in the LORD and do good; dwell in the land and enjoy safe pasture. Take delight in the LORD, and he will give you the desires of your heart. Commit your way to the LORD; trust in him and he will do this" (Psalm 37:3-5). Now observe what the Scriptures say of those whose trust is in God.

"Blessed (happy) is the one who takes refuge in Him" (Psalm 34:8). "Blessed (happy) are those whose help is the God of Jacob, whose hope is in the LORD their God" (Psalm 146:5).

What a vista of happiness is open to us, in a constant, faithful trust in Him! May it be ours ever to be seeking this added joy! We knew very little of Christ in our early days as Christians, but we love to read our Bibles to seek to learn more of Him. Gradually with the help of the Holy Spirit we learned of Him, and each fresh revelation was an added joy, as we saw new beauties, new glories in Him. Perhaps we felt something of what Peter must have felt when the Lord said to him, "Blessed (happy) are you, Simon son of Jonah, for this was not revealed to you by flesh and blood, but by my Father in heaven" (Matthew 16:17). And so every little we learned added to our joy. Not only did we learn Christ as Saviour, we learned that He is also our Lord. The fact that we must now follow Him was coupled with deep searchings of heart. We read His own words, "Blessed (happy) are they that hear the word of God, and keep it" (Luke 11:28) and again, "Now that you know these things, you will be blessed (happy) if you do them" (John 13:17).

James knew something of this when he gave us the delightful illustration of the man and the mirror (James 1:22-25). "Do not merely listen to the word, and so deceive yourselves. Do what it says. Anyone who listens to the word but does not do what it says is like someone who looks at his face in a mirror and, after looking at himself, goes away and immediately forgets what he looks like. But whoever looks intently into the perfect law that gives freedom, and continues in it - not forgetting what they have heard, but doing it - they will be blessed in what they do." The Lord has always laid great emphasis on doing.

We all remember the great Bible reading of Nehemiah 8. What searchings of heart were there then! Men and women stood and listened to the reading of the Scriptures: "They read from the Book of the Law of God, making it clear and giving the meaning so that the people understood what was being read. (verse 8). "For all the people had been weeping as they listened to the words of the Law" (verse 9). "Then all the people went away to eat and drink, to send portions of food and to celebrate with great joy, because they now understood the words that had been made known to them" (verse 12). When they observed to do, "there was very great gladness." What a happy people!

The day came when we learned the truth of baptism, and as we pondered the Lord's commandments, perhaps the words of the Lord came to mind, "Blessed (happy) are you if you do them." We learned by experience the truth of His words by being obedient. It was thus, step by step, we began to realize that the river of His pleasures was an expanding experience. We were drinking of its sweet waters as we were able.

When we were baptized, a new life opened to us. We had openly made known that we were the Lord's disciples. Our allegiance was to

Him, and we should walk even as He walked. This was going to cost something! It called for separation from the world, its pleasures and plans (1 John 2:15-17). It cut across friendship with the world (James 4:4), for bad company corrupts good character (1 Corinthians 15:38), and our friends were to be from then on like those of the psalmist, "I am a friend to all who fear you, to all who follow your precepts" (Psalm 119:63).

There is no joy in disobedience. Wisdom says, "Blessed (happy) are they that keep My ways" (Proverbs 8:82). Let us drink here and heed Wisdom's voice for, "Blessed (happy) is the one who does not walk in step with the wicked or stand in the way that sinners take or sit in the company of mockers, but whose delight is in the law of the LORD, and who meditates on his law day and night" (Psalm 1:1-2). "Blessed (happy) are all who fear the Lord, who walk in obedience to Him" (Psalm 128:1).

True happiness is found in willing obedience, our conforming to the will of God, even though it costs much, for we are reminded that "everyone who wants to live a godly life in Christ Jesus will be persecuted" (2 Timothy 3:12). We have to reckon with the evil one who, though he cannot destroy our life in Christ, will nevertheless seek to destroy our life for Christ. Not only so, but God at times permits us to pass through times of difficulty, to prove us. We may not understand why we should suffer, especially when we are seeking to do the will of God, and to walk in His ways, and to honour Him. Think it not strange because Christ also suffered in this way, for "Christ suffered for you, leaving you an example, that you should follow in his steps" (1 Peter 2:21).

These were not His sufferings for sin. We could never follow Him in that, but He did suffer for righteousness' sake. That is where we sometimes find ourselves and God permits it (1 Peter 3:17). Don't be downcast. The scripture says, "But even if you should suffer for what is right, you are blessed (happy). (1 Peter 3:14). "If you are insulted because of the name of Christ, you are blessed (happy), for the Spirit of glory and of God rests on you." (1 Peter 4:14).

Perhaps none of the Lord's servants suffered so much as Paul, and what a happy man he was! Through it all, imprisonments, scourgings and so forth, he remained unswerving in his loyalty to His beloved Lord. He loved the Lord's things and he loved the Lord's people. He was prepared to suffer; others also counted it an honour (Acts 5:41). He wrote, "I rejoice in what I am suffering for you" (Colossians 1:24). I am greatly encouraged; in all our troubles my joy knows no bounds" (2 Corinthians 7:4). These waters may seem bitter, but afterwards they yield deep, lasting joy. May we, too, be counted worthy to suffer.

5: COMMUNION - THE JOY OF THE BURNING HEART

Someone has said that the Bible is a book of promises. There is much truth in that and the more we read it, the more promises we shall find. Many of the promises of the Bible become ours only when we accept them by faith. The promise of communion is found in Revelation 3:20. Some parts of Revelation are not easy to understand, but there is a promise in it given to all who read and obey the book's message (1:3). Don't fail to read the book or you will miss the blessing of that promise: "Behold I stand at the door and knock: if any man hear My voice and open the door, I will come in to him, and sup with him, and he with Me".

The Lord Jesus was speaking here to some poor, lukewarm Christians. Such Christians have no real joy in the Lord. They do not witness for Him, nor praise His Name. They are powerless and fruitless, all because they do not have communion with Christ. The Lord sends a message through His servant John to tell them that He was standing knocking at the door of their hearts, and if they would only open He would come in and have fellowship with them. What a great promise that was! And the promise is to us also, and to Christians everywhere.

Christian, don't be lukewarm. Make sure every day that you ask the Lord to come and dwell with you and sup with you. Whatever else you forget to ask, don't forget to ask for His presence with you. Remember the story about the two disciples who met the Lord on the way to Emmaus, and how when He walked and talked with them, their hearts burned within them and how they hurried back about seven miles to tell the other disciples they had seen the Lord and how He had talked with them. That was real communion; no wonder their hearts burned within them.

Be a Christian with a burning heart, don't be lukewarm. True joy comes from within, not from without. When we have burning hearts, this will be seen in our faces, our actions and our words. Those who have burning hearts will overflow like the Psalmist in Psalm 45:1. His heart overflowed because he was thinking about the King, that is about the Lord Jesus.

What a delightful thing it is to meet disciples who have burning hearts - those who overflow to others because the Lord is with them! Fellow-believer, do you belong to the "Order of the Burning Heart?" Why not join this company today? Claim the promise of Revelation 3:20 and ask the Master to come and be at home with you. And He will, every day, when you ask Him.

But you must, of course, put out of your life all the things that are unworthy of His presence. There should be no "filthiness, nor foolish talking, or jesting ... but rather giving of thanks" (Ephesians 5:4); no uncleanness or unworthy books or magazines; We must have a real spring-cleaning of these. No joining with the world in its vain amusements. "As He is, even so are we in this world" (1 John 4:17).

Yes, that helps us to know what to do, and where to go.

And then the yielded life. Remember the story of the servant who chose rather to serve his master than to go out free (Exodus 21:2-6). Read it again today, and think of yourself as the servant and the Lord Jesus as your Master. When all is ready, and our hearts are yielded and clean, we can invite the Master to come; and every day, and all the days, He will come. Then our lives will be full and abundant and overflowing, because He is at home with us. This is communion. This is the joy of the burning heart. Then, in the joy of fellowship with Him, we can go out and serve Him, for fellowship in secret leads to fellowship in service. Press on in this, for your life can be a very real blessing to many others.

6: HALLELUJAH – THE JOY OF HEAVEN

The word Hallelujah has come into the English language through its use in the Scriptures. It is an untranslated Hebrew word meaning "Praise ye Jah" or "Praise ye the Lord". It had an important place in the service of song used in the temple of old, in Jerusalem. It enshrines the ultimate divine purpose in God's dealing in grace with men, as it is written "that we should be unto the praise of His glory" or "to the praise of the glory of His grace" (Ephesians 1:12,6). The words of the heavenly host, "Glory to God in the highest, and on earth peace" (Luke 2:14) set forth the same truth as they announced the coming of One whose name was called "Immanuel ... God with us". Note here that God's glory comes first, then man's blessing. The words of the Lord agree with this: "I have brought you glory on earth by finishing the work you gave me to do" (John 17:4).

The word Hallelujah occurs frequently in the later psalms, reaching a crescendo in the last five psalms, where all creation is called upon to "Praise the LORD". But it is not these great outbursts of praise that we have before us now, but the glorious event recorded in Revelation

19 where we find the only Hallelujahs mentioned in the New Testament. This at once impresses the mind with the transcendent importance of the occasion when they are uttered. A grand climax of heavenly joy is expressed when "the Lamb" who is seen in chapter 5 "in the midst of the throne", at last sees of the travail of His soul and is satisfied. The same blessed Person was seen on earth as "the Lamb of God" bearing away the sin of the world, "in the midst" crowned with thorns, between two robbers! What a wonderful contrast between that scene at Golgotha and the scene depicted in Revelation 19.1-6!

"But now He reigns with glory crowned,
While angel hosts the throne surround,
And still His lofty praises sound."

"Oh! what a vast immeasurable span,
'Twixt glorious Godhead, and this death as Man
'Twixt throne of God, and this detested cross;
Mind is astounded, reason at a loss;
Nor can conceive how One so high as He,
For creature's sins, should suffer on the tree."

Immediately preceding the scene of majestic glory and praise ("I heard as it were a great multitude in heaven, saying Hallelujah" says verse 1), we are directed to a scene on earth with a most sombre background - a great outpouring of divine judgements. The world's religion, commerce, science, and politics are all seen coming to their appointed end (Revelation 17ff.). The finality of these things is stated in the words, "no more at all", repeated seven times. Unutterably sad is the cry, "Woe, woe" (18:10,16,19). Words wrung from the hearts of those whose all has been built upon the sand foundation of "Babylon the great" (18:2).

The dark climax of all this is seen in Revelation 18:23, which begins, "The light of a lamp will never shine in you again." When war was declared in August 1914, Sir Edward Grey, the Foreign Secretary, said,

"The lights are going out all over Europe tonight." I still recall the feeling of dread that crept over me as I read those words. The lights were out for four years. But here, in Revelation 18, there is no recovery: it is the end. "The voice of bridegroom and bride will never be heard in you again." The joys and pleasures of Babylon are finished!

Such is the background to the scene of rapturous joy and praise. "A great multitude" is seen, and a mighty outburst of praise is expressed in the word Hallelujah! The basis of this great outburst of praise is the "true and righteous" judgements of God. "And a second time they say, Hallelujah." And then those wonderful beings, nearest to the throne, "fell down and worshipped God that sitteth on the throne, saying, Amen; Hallelujah". Can there be anything more rapturous, more glorious than this? Yes, a voice came forth from the throne, saying, Give praise to our God, all ye His servants, ye that fear Him, the small and the great". We reverently ask, whose voice can this be? We suggest, none other than the voice of Him who, when He had purged our sins, sat down on the right hand of the Majesty on high. Notice the words, "Give praise to our God". Here, surely, is the great princely Leader of our praises, the One who said in the prophetic words of Psalm 22, "in the midst of the assembly I will praise You," and, "From You comes the theme of praise in the great assembly" (22,25).

All, all are called upon to join in this final supreme anthem, "the small and the great", for THE MARRIAGE OF THE LAMB IS COME. Hallelujah! Here we reach the pinnacle of heavenly praise. Rising from the depths of joyful hearts, "fulness of joy" finds rapturous expression. On earth we sing, joyfully,

"Sing the Son's unbounded love,
How He left the realms above
To rejoin the Father's side
With a blood-bought spotless Bride."

But earth never knew such a song as this. John, the Seer, tries to illustrate from the phenomena of nature something of that grand and glorious sound: "I heard as it were the voice of many waters, and as the voice of mighty thunders, saying, Hallelujah." Why? "For the marriage of the Lamb is come." O, glorious compensation for the lonely Man of Golgotha, when indeed in fullest measure "He shall see of the travail of His soul and shall be satisfied"!

The psalm of the King (Psalm 45) points to that day: "All your garments are fragrant with myrrh, and aloes, and cassia; from palaces adorned with ivory the music of strings has makes You glad ... at Your right hand is the royal bride in gold of Ophir" (verses 8,9). How sweetly are revealed the thoughts of His heart, reminding us of Paul's words, "Christ also loved the Church, and gave Himself up for it ... that He might present the Church to Himself a glorious Church, not having spot or wrinkle or any such thing; but that it should be holy and without blemish" (Ephesians 5:25-27)!

And when the last lights are going out on earth, and the last words of bride and bridegroom have been spoken here, then will begin the endless joy and song of heaven. True, "On earth the song begins", but we await the day when we shall join in the:

"Blest anthem of eternal days,
The fulness of the rapt'rous song
To Christ the Saviour's endless praise."

Well, indeed, may Peter speak of "joy unspeakable and full of glory"!

"When the praise of heaven I hear,
Loud as thunders to the ear,
Loud as many waters noise,
Sweet as harp's melodious voice;
Then, Lord, shall I fully know,
Not till then how much I owe.

7: THE JOY OF PSALMS 42 & 43

These two Psalms express the experience of a Levite who was engaged in the service of song within the house of God. They reveal the joy that fills the heart of those who engage in worship.

The Psalms are a Maschil - that which is for instruction - of the sons of Korah who were of the Levitical family of the Kohathites (Exodus 6:16,18,21). Their charge in the service of God during the wilderness journey was the ark, the table of showbread, the lampstand, the altars, and the vessels of the sanctuary (Numbers 3:29-31). These were carried on their shoulders throughout the years spent by the nation in the desert (Numbers 1:50; 3:7-9). The cities which were given to them by lot out of the tribes of Israel were at least twenty-three in number (Joshua 21:4,5). It was probably in the territory of the tribe of Dan that the experience of the Psalmist took place (Psalm 42:6).

When king David made arrangements for the service of song in the house of God he appointed among others, certain of the Kohathites, namely Heman and Asaph (1 Chronicles 6:33,39). We find them mentioned again when Solomon brought the ark of the covenant into the temple. The many musical instruments which the Levites used in praising the Lord are also mentioned (2 Chronicles 5:12,13). The man who wrote Psalm 43 was one whose responsibility in praise included the use of the harp.

Worship is at the heart of these two Psalms. The Psalmist's meditation concerns his experiences in the past, what he is passing through in the present, and his hope for the coming day when he will again appear before God. He recalled former days when with others of a kindred heart he went to engage in worship at the house of God. These occasions were marked by a deep sense of joy in praise, times when he knew refreshment within his whole being. As he worshipped, he drank deep of the river of God. Days had now changed. There were tears both day and night. He was conscious of a void and a thirst within himself. He vents his feelings in these words, "As the hart panteth ..." We imagine the hart in the wilderness longing to slake its thirst in the cool waters, but unable to find such a place. So did the Psalmist pant, longing for God, thirsting for Him, for God alone could quench the dryness within.

The cry from his heart reveals his depression. "Why, my soul, are you downcast? Why so disturbed within me?" Three times he uttered this cry. His distress was great. He longed for the day when he could say "Return to your rest, my soul, for the LORD has been good to you" (Psalm 116:7). What was the cause of such anxiety? Two reasons are clear which resulted in this breakdown of communion with God.

In Psalm 42:6-7 we picture the Psalmist standing on the hill Mizar which is among the foothills of Mount Hermon from where the Jordan has its source. (The tribe of Dan had their inheritance in this part. They also possessed territory on the coast, lying between the tribes of Ephraim and Judah – see Joshua 19:40-48). Looking toward Jerusalem, listening to the rushing sound of the water of Jordan (at the time of the harvest its banks would overflow – see Joshua 3:15), the thoughts of his heart are expressed, "Deep calls to deep in the roar of your waterfalls. All your waves and breakers have swept over me."

These words are similar to what a prophet of God would utter because of sin (Jonah 2:3). He felt desolate by reason of personal failure and the chastening hand of God. Oppression of enemies is mentioned in Psalm 42:9-10 and Psalm 43:2. Their character is revealed as ungodly, deceitful and unjust. Now restricted by his adversaries, without any likelihood of deliverance, he feels forgotten and cast off. They reproach him with their constant taunting, "Where is your God?" Although he is in this dismayed state yet he looks forward to the day when, once again he will praise God, who is the health of his countenance.

His prayer then in Psalm 43 is for deliverance and guidance, "Vindicate me ... plead my cause ... rescue me". This is the earnest request of the person committing everything into the hand of God, confident of God's righteous judgement against deceit and injustice. This leads to the darkness giving place to light and truth which lead to God's holy hill and His dwelling place. There is the altar of God, where activity centred in God, who is the gladness of joy, brings spiritual enjoyment. The joy of the Lord would be his strength. The praise of the Lord would be the source of that joy.

The house of God and its worship should be very precious to His people today as in the past. The fulfilment of responsibility in the service of praise will also bring that joy which filled the hearts of godly men of old. There will be occasions when by reason of failure and other circumstances our desire and ability to worship will be hindered, perhaps leading to a depression of soul known by the Psalmist. We cry, "Why, my soul, are you downcast?" Then we must remember also his confidence - "Put your hope in God, for I will yet praise Him".

8: DELIGHT IN THE LORD

There can be no doubt that, before the Fall, Adam and Eve found all their delight and joy in God and in doing His will. Nothing else engaged their interest except God and His creation. With the advent of sin this was reversed; the effects of evil soon became evident. Both divine verdict and human experience agree that man in his fallen state seeks only to satisfy the desires of his flesh and mind, taking pleasure in unrighteousness and delighting in things hateful to God (Isaiah 66:3). The restless longing of his soul finds no interest, far less joy, in contemplating his Creator or in the spiritual things of eternal value found in Christ at the right hand of God (Colossians 3:1-2).

Back in the distant days of Job, it was recognized that the godless man would not delight himself in the Almighty nor call upon Him (Job 27:10). The words of Eliphaz were sound advice for Job and for all the godly who come after him, "Submit to God and be at peace with him ... then you will find delight in the Almighty and will lift up your face to God" (Job 22:21,26). The deep satisfaction and inward joy of real delight in God were not peculiar to the age in which Job and his friends lived. The psalmist also found God and His word the most gratifying object of his life, "Your testimonies also are my delight"; "I will delight myself in Your commandments which I have loved"; "Your law is my delight"; "Your commandments are my delight". Learning the law of God and obeying it brought greater pleasure to the psalmist than anything else.

It is fitting to ask ourselves - do we find delight and inward pleasure in the law of God? Do we prefer before every other earthly engagement to sit down and meditate profitably on the Scriptures of truth? Or is our reading of God's word a dry formality that we try to complete as quickly as possible? If Christ has the right place in our affections, and if our minds are properly focused on things eternal, then our reading of God's word and the doing of His law will be a joy and delight to our souls, a feast of spiritual food without which we cannot grow or increase in spiritual stature.

It is sad in the extreme when the word of God has lost its appeal to God's saints. This is an obvious symptom of a low spiritual condition such as existed in Israel when in the wilderness they lusted for the food of Egypt and confessed, "Our soul is dried away; there is nothing at all: we have nought save this manna to look to" (Numbers 11:6).

They did not look to the manna for sustenance and strength. In their unbelief and lust they treated with disdain the bread of the Mighty and looked back to the foods they had eaten in Egypt for free, deliberately forgetting that they paid dearly in affliction and oppression for all they obtained there. Surely it's true to say there are no bargains in Egypt or in the world which it represents. If we prefer to have our interest and delight in the things of this world we shall have to pay for it in full, if not now, certainly at the judgement seat of Christ. Nothing so dries up the soul as longing after the things of earth. What a contrast is the man whose delight is in the law of the Lord, "That person is like a tree planted by streams of water, which yields its fruit in season and whose leaf does not wither - whatever they do prospers (Psalm 1:3).

The interest of man was never provided for on such a scale as it is at the present time. All the inventions and discoveries of our age coupled with the affluence which modern society affords are skilfully arranged to delight the insatiable desires of the human heart and to attract the interest of people of all ages. Things of this world both legitimate and trivial can be a real barrier between God and men, and can easily blight the life of a believer unless treated with the utmost caution. Possessions, pleasures and pastimes can become a devouring obsession of faculty and time, if allowed to intrude on one's spiritual life. Hence the warning, "Love not the world, neither the things that are in the world ..." (1 John 2:15). The apostle Paul has recorded for our warning the sad case of Demas (2 Timothy 4:10), who although saved by grace and gifted by the ascended Christ for the service of God, nevertheless succumbed to the gravitating influence of worldly things.

In his time on earth, the Lord Jesus found all His pleasure in doing His Father's will, He fulfilled the prophetic scripture "I delight to do Your will, O My God; and Your law is within My heart" (Psalm 40:8 NKJV). May God give us grace to seek our delight in the Lord and in His law, that we might be able to say, "I sat down under his shadow with great delight, and his fruit was sweet to my taste" (Song of Songs 2:3).

9: LAUGHTER AND TEARS

Isaac - his name means 'laughter'; a name chosen by God before his birth. For Sarah, his ninety-year old mother, had laughed sceptically when she overheard the Angel of the LORD tell Abraham that he would have a son by her. Now with the promised infant in her arms she said, "God has made me laugh, and all who hear will laugh with me" (Genesis 21:6). Abraham's household rejoiced: their mouth was 'filled with laughter', and their 'tongue with singing' as one psalmist described overflowing joy (Psalm 126:2).

A child of promise, a child of destiny, Isaac thrived in Sarah's tender love and under his father's watchful care. What joy would fill their hearts with each delightful stage of Isaac's growth through infancy, to his first faltering steps, and then to see him after the manner of toddlers inquisitively exploring the ins and outs of the richly appointed encampment.

Laughter and tears! It could not be joy and sunshine all the way. Nor can it be for any of us. We learn from Bible illustration the deep wisdom of God, His purposes in the mingling of laughter and tears in experience with Him: a truth reflected in Anne Proctor's perceptive lines:

We thank Thee more, that all our joy
Is touched with pain,
That shadows fall on brightest hours,
That thorns remain;
So that earth's bliss may be our guide,
And not our chain.

It was a joyful occasion when Isaac was weaned. Abraham made a great feast that day. Sadly, things were soured through Sarah's drawing attention to Ishmael's mocking of Isaac, and her harsh demand that Hagar and Ishmael should be expelled: "Cast out this bondwoman and her son; for the son of this bondwoman shall not be heir with my son, *namely* with Isaac" (Genesis 21:10). How deeply distressing to Abraham that his older son, now probably about seventeen, should have to be banished. He anguished over it before the LORD, but was told to concede Sarah's demand. Graciously, God showed His servant that the choice of Isaac as the son in whom special divine purpose was vested made Ishmael's departure necessary. Nevertheless, from Ishmael, too, there would arise a nation, because he was Abraham's seed.

Early in the morning Abraham gave effect to God's direction. As he watched mother and son disappear forlornly into the unknown, were his eyes dim with tears? Were Hagar and Ishmael also weeping as they felt the wrench of alienation from accustomed family and friends? How often, when laughter has turned to tears, we need to cling implicitly to the promises of God. As one who knew bitter experiences of mental stress exhorts in his well-known hymn:

Judge not the Lord by feeble sense,
But trust Him for His grace;
Behind a frowning providence
He hides a smiling face.
Blind unbelief is sure to err,
And scan His work in vain;
God is His own interpreter,
And He will make it plain. (W. Cowper)

10: JOY IN GIVING

The Christian is a new man with new thoughts (2 Corinthians 5:17). He has learned that life consists, not merely of receiving, but of giving, as the Lord Jesus said, "It is more blessed to give than to receive" (Acts 20:85). As to ourselves, the Scripture says, "You are not your own; you were bought at a price" (1 Corinthians 6:19,20). This is the foundation of all Christian giving, and the servant of Christ must yield himself to his Master, because he has been bought with His blood. Delivered from eternal death, he must now live unto Christ, who for his sake died and rose again (2 Corinthians 5:14,15).

This is the beginning of Christian service. We read of the believers in Macedonia, that "first they gave themselves to the Lord" (2 Corinthians 8:1-5). Because they had first given themselves to the Lord, they then joyfully gave of their substance. The servant of Christ will learn from this. Happy is the man who has ceased to please himself, so that he can please Christ! That man has found true rest. When we have given ourselves with joy to God, we shall begin to experience the joy of giving our substance. David expressed the joy of this giving in 1 Chronicles 29. The servant of Christ should ponder this chapter well. Here we find the true heart of David revealed. After giving his all to God, he said, "Everything comes from you, and we have given you only what comes from your hand" (verse 14). This is the true secret of giving, and the servant of Christ must learn it well. The portion of our substance that we give to the Lord will often be an indication to ourselves (for others will not know it) of the true measure of our love to the Lord. Giving to the Lord will wonderfully increase our joy in the Lord.

Our giving to the Lord should be a definite portion of our income, it should not be given at random. The servant of Christ should give what he has decided in his heart to give remembering that God is able to make all grace abound unto him (2 Corinthians 9:7, 8). He should also give "as he may prosper." The more he receives from the Lord, so much the more should he set apart to be given again to Him on the first day of the week (1 Corinthians 16:2).

In the Old Testament, God's people were commanded to give the tithe (tenth) of all that God gave them (Leviticus 27). The Levites who received the tithe from the people, were to give to God, the tithe of what they received (Numbers 18:24-26). In so giving they were honouring God, from whom they had received all. The Lord promised to bless the people when they brought the whole tithe to Him (Malachi 3:10). God has not commanded us to bring any fixed portion today, but what He asked in the Old Testament has been a guide to many, and they have been blessed in so giving. We read in 2 Corinthians 9:6, 7 that "He that sows generously will also reap generously" and, "God loves a cheerful giver." The servant of Christ should be careful to honour the Lord in this way (Proverbs 3:9,10).

It is not only in giving a portion of what we receive, that we can glorify God; we can become His channels of giving to others. What we have, has been given to us so that we can use it in His service. It is evident that this is God's will for us. Only as we realize that we are the channels of God's giving, can He freely pour through us to others as He would. "Freely you have received, freely give," the Lord said to His apostles (Matthew 10:8). This is the lesson of the loaves. "Where could we get enough bread in this remote place to feed such a crowd?" said the disciples (Matthew 15:33). Where indeed unless they were provided by the Lord: The only limit of their giving was His resources, and they were limitless! Foolish disciples! To think that His great work among men could be limited to their small resources! Their resources, like their thoughts, were small indeed.

So also are ours, until we realize that our giving is not really ours at all, but His giving through us. Only the tiniest part of the heat energy given forth from the Sun is used on the earth, and yet it sustains all the physical life here. Our Maker thus shows us something of His limitless resources in His creation. O servant of Christ, yield yourself unreservedly to Him, so that He may pour out again through you what He would give to others!

Let us remember that at the most we can only be the channels of the blessing of God to others. Whether it be in the truth of God that He has shown us, or in the substance that He has given us, let it flow freely through us to others, for, "It is more blessed to give than to receive." Remember the promise, "Give, and it shall be given unto you; good measure ..." (Luke 6:38).

11: THE OIL OF JOY

From whatever angle, and in whatever circumstances, we may view our great Redeemer, we may see fresh beauties and radiations of His glory. There is nothing that He has done, or will yet do, that will not display something of the Divine glory which uniquely belongs to Himself, and in which also are manifestations of the Godhead. It is a soul-satisfying thought that God has found in Him what satisfies the deep longings of His own heart for all eternity.

There is no requirement of God's holy throne that has not found its perfect answer in the perfect life and Cross-work of our Lord Jesus Christ, and there is no longing in God's heart of infinite love that has not found its full response and satisfaction in the Person of Christ. With joy we may exult and say: "Look on our shield, O God, look with favour on Your anointed one" (Psalm 84:9).

"To Him be the glory both now and for ever. Amen." Indeed if this were not so, there could be no outpouring of blessing upon men. It was only when God had received His portion from the sacrifices on Israel's altars that they could receive the blessings and benefits. God has found in the accomplished work of Calvary and the glorious triumph of resurrection, eternal delight. He can with joy look upon the Man of His right hand, upon the Son of Man whom He made strong for Himself, "The Man that is My Fellow." From the terrors, horrors and darkness of the cross and tomb, God has raised Him up. He has seated Him at His own right hand, and of Him it is prophetically written, "You will fill me with joy in your presence" (Acts 2:28).

He had known the bitter loneliness of being forsaken by God, the hiding of God's face, the unanswered cry in the experience of His deepest distress when it was fulfilled, "... the Lord makes His soul an offering for sin" (Isaiah 53:10).

"The head once full of bruises,
So full of pain and scorn,
Midst other sore abuses
Mocked with a crown of thorn.
That head is now surrounded
With brightest majesty,
In death once bowed and wounded,
Accursed on the tree."

Yes, the crucified One is now the enthroned One, the everlasting doors have been opened for the return of the triumphant Saviour. He has been "received up in glory," and of the Son God says, "Your throne, O God, will last for ever and ever; a scepter of justice will be the scepter of your kingdom. You have loved righteousness and hated wickedness; therefore God, your God, has set you above your companions by anointing you with the oil of joy" (Hebrews 1:9).

Two things are said about making Christ glad. He was made glad with the Father's countenance, and He was anointed with the oil of joy (gladness) by the Father. It rejoices our hearts to think that the lonely

Sufferer of Calvary has been made glad with the countenance of His Father, He has looked upon the battle-scarred returning Conqueror with infinite delight and approval. What joy filled the heart of the Father! What a wealth of meaning is conveyed by the countenance! It speaks volumes without words.

For the Son to look upon the face of His Father which conveyed such unspeakable pleasure, filled Him with the fullness of gladness. As Psalm 16:11 says, "In Your presence is fullness of joy; At your right hand are pleasures for evermore." Thus we see the blessed or happy God rejoicing over the Son of His love in the knowledge that all had been completed, the basis had been laid whereby all God's future purposes of grace could righteously be accomplished. He had truly loved righteousness, even though it had involved Him in untold suffering and reproach. Nothing could or did cause Him to deviate from the paths of righteousness in the slightest degree, and in this He had found delight.

"I delight to do Your will, O My God" was the language of His heart. He was that blessed or happy Man of Psalm 1 who delighted in the law of the LORD; and in His law did He meditate day and night. There was no happier Man on earth than He, He was possessed of an inward joy, and a calm unruffled peace within, which was known to no other. He was the perfect hearer, and fulfiller of God's law and will. He could say, "I have glorified You on the earth. I have finished the work which You have given Me to do" (John 17:4).

Now the Father shows His approbation and makes Him glad with His countenance, "The light of the eyes rejoices the heart" (Proverbs 15:30 NKJV). Moreover, in association with His throne and sceptre He was anointed with the oil of joy above His fellows. It is said in Proverbs 27:9 that "Ointment and perfume rejoice the heart." After referring to this wondrous occasion, the Psalmist then says, "All your robes are fragrant with myrrh and aloes and cassia; from palaces adorned with ivory the music of the strings makes you glad." (Psalm 45:8). And who more worthy than He to be made glad!

"Then I looked and heard the voice of many angels, numbering thousands upon thousands, and ten thousand times ten thousand. They encircled the throne and the living creatures and the elders. In a loud voice they were saying: "Worthy is the Lamb, who was slain, to receive power and wealth and wisdom and strength and honor and glory and praise!" (Revelation 5:11-12)

All heaven acclaims His worthiness, and of all in that holy, happy land, there is now none so radiant with joy as He, and all heaven rejoices in the honour bestowed upon their King and Redeemer. Never again will He be called upon to go out alone into the darkness and storms of a cruel, God-hating world to suffer. With joy we can now sing,

"'Tis past, the dark and dreary night,
O God, we see Him now,
Our morning Star, without a cloud
Of sadness on His brow."

Why should His people then be sad? Should we not catch the spirit of that anointing scene in heaven and rejoice greatly with joy unspeakable and full of glory? Should we not be displaying on earth something of the joyousness of Christ's triumphant gladness? Our Saviour is a rejoicing Christ upon the throne, and we through Him have received "The oil of joy for mourning, the garment of praise for the spirit of heaviness." It is ours with joy to draw water out of the wells of salvation, and say with the psalmist, "May we shout for joy over your victory and lift up our banners in the name of our God" (Psalm 20:5).

Being a Christian is not a miserable, long-faced, sanctimonious profession, it is a joyous life to be known and lived in like kind to Christ's. May we so live and act that others may see in us this joy, so that they, like the Queen of Sheba, may testify truly, "How happy your people must be! How happy your officials, who continually stand before you and hear your wisdom" (1 Kings 10:8).

Have we not known the happiness of the one "whose transgressions are forgiven, whose sins are covered"? (Psalm 32:1) And also the happiness of the man who is chosen and brought near to live in his courts (Psalm 65:4)? Have we not been comforted in Zion, the place of God's choice? And have we not found it to be a place "the garden of the LORD. Joy and gladness will be found in her, thanksgiving and the sound of singing" (Isaiah 51:3)? Therefore, "Rejoice in the Lord always. I will say it again, Rejoice." (Philippians 4:4).

12: INFELICISSIMUS

P eople in days gone by used this Latin word to describe their miserable condition. It means "most unhappy." It was once placed on the tombstone of a great philosopher at his own request, and this can easily be understood, for the man lived and died without Christ. But "infelicissimus" should never be used of a child of God, though sad to say it can be.

As believers on the Lord Jesus Christ we cannot lose our salvation. "I give unto them (My sheep) eternal life; and they shall never perish, and no one shall snatch them out of My hand" (John 10:28) is sufficient proof of this, for the guarantee was given by the Lord Himself. But we can lose the joy of our salvation. This can happen to "the best" of saved persons; to young or old. It happened to David, and caused him to cry out to the Lord: "Restore to me the joy of your salvation and grant me a willing spirit, to sustain me. Then I will teach transgressors your ways, so that sinners will turn back to you" (Psalm 51:12,13).

What had happened to the man after God's heart? He had sinned. When he should have been out fighting the battles of the LORD he remained at home. Temptation overtook him. He not only took another man's wife, but also ruthlessly planned the man's death (see 2 Samuel 11). David tried to live with this sin on his conscience, but it was impossible. His spiritual strength would ebb away day by day. He was like the eagle that swooped to the earth to gather its prey, and a serpent buried its fangs into the bird's body. It held on grimly as the giant bird rose as before to greet heights in the heavens, but the eagle gradually found its strength failing. It found it could not rise as high as it had done before; the more it tried the less it succeeded and soon it found itself descending unwillingly to the earth to die from the enemy's poison.

David could not rise to any spiritual heights while sin lurked in his bosom. Neither can I nor you. It will keep us earthbound spiritually as it did David. He was no longer able to serve the LORD with "clean hands, and a pure heart," and a soul not lifted up unto vanity (Psalm 24:4). He confessed to God, "For I know my transgressions, and my sin is always before me. Against you, you only, have I sinned and done what is evil in your sight" (Psalm 51:3-4).

David had lost the joy of his salvation. He was "infelicissimus." What was the way back? How could David know restoration? It was by way of confession, repentance, and cleansing. Read again Psalm 51. For I know my transgressions" (verse 3). "Cleanse me with hyssop, and I shall be clean: Wash me, and I will be 'whiter than snow" (verse 7). "Create in me a pure heart, O God; and renew a steadfast spirit within me" (verse 10).

What agony of soul this man of God went through after the joy of God's salvation had departed from him because of sin! What a warning to us as men and women of God today! For how easy it is for sin to rob us of our joy in the Lord, and to nullify our service for Him! There are so many things that can creep in to bring this about, such as doubtful associations, undesirable literature, unkind remarks about our brethren and sisters, unclean thoughts, jealousies. Encouraging these things in our lives is just like the beginning of David's mistake in "staying at home," when he should be fighting the battles of the Lord.

Our warfare, says the apostle Paul, is against the world rulers of this darkness and against the spiritual hosts of wickedness. (Ephesians 6:10-20). Let us put on the whole armour of God and be worthy soldiers of the Lord Jesus; let us rejoice fully in the knowledge of His wonderful salvation; let us be happy in His service, that the words spoken by the Queen of Sheba to Solomon might also apply to us as servants of the Lord Jesus: "How happy your people must be …!" (1 Kings 10).

13: THE JOY OF THANKSGIVING

Rooted and builded up in Him ... overflowing with thankfulness" (Colossians 2:7).

Among the characteristics of the last days is that men will be unthankful" and "unholy". These are very evident in our day. The giving of thanks is a godly trait, and not only is it right that we should be thankful, but it has a very positive effect upon our whole man, spirit and soul and body.

Thanksgiving was one of the causes of David's fruitful life. It comes out again and again in his life and writings. How much we owe to David for the outpourings of his heart! One of the lessons the servant of Christ must learn is that overflowing in thankfulness. It may be easy for the Christian to give thanks when things go well with him. He will seldom fail to do so, for he knows that every perfect gift is from above (James 1:17). But overflowing in thankfulness will take us far beyond that. When Paul wrote this, he was a prisoner in Rome! How well he had learnt the lesson and how fruitful a life he lived! We also can learn it, and overflow in thankfulness, for "Jesus Christ is the same yesterday and today, yes and for ever" (Hebrews 13:8). What He was to His faithful servants in the past, He will be to us also as we overflow in thanksgiving.

1 Chronicles 29 is a very revealing chapter in the life of David, and His words are a tonic to us today. In his lifetime, David amassed very great wealth, but he gladly gave it all for God's dwelling place, and he gave thanks that he was privileged to do so! That is spiritual maturity. It was not the giving of thanks that he had received so much, but that he was privileged to be able to give so much! This is what he said: "Now, our God, we give you thanks, and praise your glorious name But who am I, and who are my people, that we should be able to give as generously as this? Everything comes from you, and we have given you only what comes from your hand" (verses 13-14).

That was thanksgiving from a heart that had learnt the greatness of God, and its own nothingness. How deeply thankful we should be that God has saved us, and called us with a holy calling! How thankful we should be that we are privileged to give ourselves and our substance to Him! In 1 Chronicles 29:22, we read, they "... ate and drank with great joy in the presence of the LORD that day". In great measure, gladness of heart is linked with thanksgiving. The unthankful heart knows little of true joy. The merriment of the world is largely a veneer that covers its lack of joy. One of the evidences of the work of the Holy Spirit within the believer is joy. Thus we read, "The fruit of the Spirit is love, joy, peace" and so forth (Galatians 5:22).

Perhaps we ought to stop and ask ourselves now: Are we filled with joy and with the Holy Spirit, as the early disciples were? Or are our lives commonplace like those of all around us? If joy is lacking and the fulness of the Spirit, let us scrutinize ourselves to see if we have failed to overflow in thankfulness. Are our prayers saturated with thanksgiving? If not then our joylessness is apparent. We have failed to overflow in thankfulness.

But are we expected to give thanks for everything? "Give thanks in all circumstances; for this is God's will for you in Christ Jesus" (1 Thessalonians 5:18). And again, "always giving thanks to God the Father for everything, in the name of our Lord Jesus Christ" (Ephesians 5:20). But many things happen to us for which we find it difficult to give thanks. Do we trust God only in the good and pleasant days? Do we not trust Him even in the dark days? Someone has written:

"When is the time to trust?
Is it when friends are true?
Is it when comforts woo
And in all we say and do
We meet but praise?
Nay but the time to trust
Is when we stand alone,
And summer birds have flown,
And every prop is gone,
All else but God."

We can trust God even when we cannot trace His way, for His way is perfect (Psalm 18:80). Let us overflow in thankfulness, and as overflow in this, the grace of God will overflow in us, and our lives, that may have become dry and commonplace, will become fresh and green, radiant with Christlikeness.

14: THE JOYFUL SOUND OF BELLS

A gold bell ... and the sound will be heard ..." (Exodus 28:35).

Sound shall be heard? What sound? Where? The sound of bells in the quiet holy place of the Tabernacle in the wilderness. It was quiet in contrast to the noise and activity of the court where the animals were brought for sacrifice on the altar of burnt offering. There would be a constant stream of victims every day to this altar to deal with sin, service, and worship. But in the holy place there would be the sounds morning and evening from the bells on the high priest's garment as he moved about in his care of the golden altar, which can speak to us of the fragrance of prayer. Also in the holy place were the golden lampstand telling of the light of testimony, and the table of showbread as a link with communion and satisfaction.

The bells sounded because they were on the hem of his robe. How pleasant that sound would be to the ear of God. Pleasant also to the people as he moved among them, for it indicated that they had a living, active high priest. The bells can also speak to us of good news, of joy; a reminder that our High Priest, the Lord Jesus, is in God's presence where He adds His sweet perfume to our prayers, reinforces our testimony in churches of God as the eternal Light, and provides full satisfaction as the Bread of God, of whom we are partakers. He fills all heaven with the joy and glory of His presence there for us; ever reminding us that we are the fruit of His toil at Calvary. Our High Priest abides for ever (Hebrews 7:24), having sat down on the right hand of the throne of the Majesty in the heavens, where He is a minister of the sanctuary (Hebrews 8:1-2).

Joyful sounds can be heard from us too, as we are exemplars of our High Priest. Time spent in the quietness of the heavenly sanctuary experiencing the joy of the Lord will enable our divine "bell" of testimony to be heard amongst His people. "And the disciples were filled with joy and with the Holy Spirit" (Acts 13:52). This is always pleasurable to God's ear as well.

15: JOY IN THE BEATITUDES - PART 1

The Sermon on the Mount was spoken during the early part of the Lord's ministry when He was very popular with the people. In fact Matthew says great multitudes followed Him from all parts of the country, and when He saw them He went up into the mountain and taught His disciples. So what He had to say was primarily to His followers, although at the end of the sermon the multitudes were astonished at His teaching - evidently they'd been listening.

"Blessed"
"Blessed are the poor in spirit, for theirs is the kingdom of heaven. Blessed are those who mourn, for they shall be comforted. Blessed are the meek, for they shall inherit the earth," and so on. It's arresting to see that the Lord Jesus began His teaching with the word blessed and repeated it nine times over. What does it mean? Happy? Yes, but more than that at least more than what the world counts as happiness. The world's happiness can be such a fleeting thing. But the happiness that the Lord Jesus gives comes from a settled peace in the heart, and it doesn't depend upon our circumstances at all. God is described in the

Bible as the blessed or happy God, and He wants us to be happy too happy with a deep sense of well-being, happy in the knowledge that our sins are forgiven and we're bound for heaven.

That's were happiness begins. "Blessed is he whose transgression is forgiven, whose sin is covered" wrote king David (Psalm 32:1), and the apostle Paul quotes his words in Romans chapter 4. And when Simon Peter confessed that the Lord Jesus was the Christ, the Son of the living God, Jesus said, "Blessed are you, Simon Bar-Jona! For flesh and blood has not revealed this to you, but my Father who is in heaven" (Matthew 16:16-17).

That's where happiness begins for any person, when he understands that the Lord Jesus is the Son of God, and for his sins and for his salvation He went to Calvary and died. The gospel Paul preached was in two parts, repentance toward God, and that comes when we are convinced of the seriousness of our sin, and faith toward our Lord Jesus Christ, and that happens when we discover as Peter did that He is the Son of the living God.

One of the happiest people I ever met was a little Chinese lady we called Aunty Hannah. She came into my life when I first went to Burma. I thank God for Aunty Hannah and what I learned from her. "Having nothing and yet possessing all things" just described her. She was so poor she could literally pack all her treasures in one small bag and carry them over her shoulder. But she was radiant with the joy of Christ and she used to spend a lot of her time visiting her many Chinese friends and telling them all about Him. Certainly she was a living proof that happiness doesn't depend on what you possess, nor upon the circumstances of your life. It's a deeper thing than that. It begins when we accept Christ as our own Saviour, and it grows as we go on to acknowledge Him as Lord.

"Blessed are the poor in spirit"

"Blessed are the poor in spirit, for theirs is the kingdom of heaven."
With these impressive words the Lord Jesus began His Sermon on the
Mount. Showing us the way to real happiness and leaving us in no
doubt whatever that this is what He desires for us so deeply, that we
should enjoy this happiness in our lives.

I suppose that's what most people in the world are searching for. If
we took a consensus of what people are wanting above anything else,
happiness would be very high on the list, I'm sure. Men and women
seek it in different ways of course in pleasure and sport, in sex, in
politics, sometimes in religion, but are they finding it? They're not, are
they? A glance through our daily newspaper convinces us of that.
They're trying so hard and failing so miserably. The real happiness that
lasts, that contentment of spirit which affects a person's whole life is
evading them. No, the world hasn't found it, hard as it has tried.

That's why I'm so thankful for the privilege of sharing with you
these words the Lord Jesus spoke, for I'm convinced with all my heart
they're the answer to the deepest need. Take time to think seriously
with me about it, please, and when you've found it yourself, pass it on
urgently to others, for time is running out and the message Jesus spoke
must be passed around the world.

"Blessed are the poor in spirit," He said, "for theirs is the kingdom
of heaven". In other words, that's how we enter the kingdom of
heaven and enjoy its lasting happiness. It's not by anything we do, nor
by any gifts that we bring. It's an attitude of heart. Blessed are the poor
in spirit. What exactly did the Lord Jesus mean by that? Certainly it's
the very opposite of what the world is advancing. If you want to get
ahead believe in yourself, the world says. Self-confidence, self-

expression, self-reliance, these are the things our youth are learning in schools and colleges. But Jesus said - and His words are undying - their truth lasts for all time - "Blessed are the poor in spirit".

What did He mean? There's a verse in Isaiah 66 which I believe sums it up. God says, "This is the man to whom I will look, he that is humble and contrite in spirit, and trembles at My word". You remember Gideon? He was a young man when God told him He was going to use him to save Israel from their enemies. His reaction is interesting. He said, "My clan is the weakest in Manasseh, and I am the least in my family". That was poverty of spirit, wasn't it? He had small thoughts about himself. To such a man God looked. He was the man God chose to use. Or think of Simon Peter. Plenty of self-confidence he had naturally, but when he came to know the Lord Jesus he fell at His knees and said, "Depart from me, for I am a sinful man, O Lord" (Luke 5:8). But the Lord didn't depart from him. Not at all. This was the very man He could use, a man who in His presence felt his own unworthiness.

And I believe that leads us right into the secret, if you can call it that, of how we become poor in spirit. The more we get acquainted with God through His Word, the less we shall think of ourselves. The more we learn of Christ, the more He will increase in our estimation, and we shall decrease. And I believe that's what He meant when He said, "Blessed are the poor in spirit, for theirs is the kingdom of heaven". So "Fix your eyes upon Jesus, look full in His glorious face, And the things of earth will grow strangely dim in the light of His glory and grace".

"Blessed are those who mourn"
In the 53rd chapter of Isaiah the Lord Jesus is described as a Man of sorrows and acquainted with grief. It's interesting we never read of

Him laughing, but we do read a few times about Him shedding tears. That doesn't mean He wasn't happy, of course. He was, sublimely so. In His parting message to His disciples He said, "These things I have spoken to you, that My joy may be in you, and that your joy may be full" (John 15:11). Like the apostle Paul, He was "sorrowful yet always rejoicing", and I believe that just opens up to us the meaning of the second beatitude: "Blessed are those who mourn, for they shall be comforted".

There may well be a word of comfort here for someone who mourns the loss of a loved one. God has a wonderful way of bringing blessing out of seeming tragedy. The Father of mercies and God of all comfort will comfort your heart in a very special way. But it will not take away from your comfort, I'm sure, if I remind you that the Lord Jesus had far more than that in mind when He spoke these words. "Blessed are those who mourn, for they shall be comforted". He was a mourner Himself. He groaned at the grave of Lazarus. "Jesus wept", is the terse way the gospel writer records it. But why? It couldn't have been because His friend Lazarus had died, for in a few minutes He was going to raise him from the dead. Nor was it only in sympathy with the sorrowing sisters, although He was undoubtedly touched by their sorrow. No, there's a deeper reason. The scripture says, "He was deeply moved in spirit and troubled". It was the effect of sin and its fearful results which troubled Him so deeply. That's why He mourned and wept.

The world laughs at sin, but God doesn't. He loathes it. On every page of His Word He calls on us to take account of the seriousness of sin. The wages of sin is death, the Bible says, and to pay its awful wages, and to free us from its power, God gave His Son in death at Calvary. That is what sin cost God. Let us never forget that. Woodrow Wilson was one of America's God-fearing presidents. He was reputed to be a man of few words. One day when he returned from church his wife asked, "What was the preacher's message today?" "Sin," he replied. "But what did he say about it?" she queried. "He was against it," said the president.

God is against sin. Men laugh about it, but God doesn't. They call it by other names. They cover it up to try and forget its seriousness. "Let us eat, drink and be merry," they say. That's a very common philosophy of life the world's prescription for happiness, but it doesn't last. Oh hear what the Lord Jesus said, "Blessed are those who mourn, for they shall be comforted". That's the way to real happiness. When we mourn over sin, that brings us to repentance and draws us back to God for forgiveness and cleansing. And there's no joy to be compared with the joy of sins forgiven. Let us make known the message that Jesus spoke. Never was it needed more urgently than today. "Blessed are those who mourn, for they shall be comforted".

16: THE STORY OF THE REEDS

They stand almost 15 feet high on the banks of eastern streams and rivers. They move with the breeze and gentle lapping of the waters. Here people came to gather the 3-inch diameter reeds which belong to the papyrus family, their flexibility being ideal for making baskets of various shapes and sizes. An anxious mother, living nearby, might have disturbed the quietness of the river area where they grew, as she gathered enough of these reeds one day to make a receptacle for the hiding of her baby boy.

A tyrant-king had issued his edict that all male babies were to be drowned; but Jochebed's child was one of destiny, a goodly child, one of special interest to God. Her fingers moved rapidly, as only a woman's can in emergencies, weaving in the secrecy of the home, a boat, or ark, that would contain her precious son. It would lie waterproofed among the very reeds from which it was made; and God's eye would be upon it. The reeds were a place of safety, for the child's life was preserved. His name, Moses, would constantly remind him when he became prince, shepherd, leader, statesman, of the preserving hand of God in his life, for it means "taken out of the water".

From these reeds of protection in the land of Egypt, for that is where Moses was born, we journey to a smaller, pretty town in the north of Israel. It is named Cana, and it is located near Nazareth in Galilee where Jesus grew up. Cana means "the place of the reeds"; one other root meaning of the name is to bend, bow, stoop, possibly taken from the appearance of the reeds growing in the area. It was at Cana of Galilee that Jesus performed His first miracle when He changed the water into wine at the wedding feast. His disciples then and now are made aware of the "good wine" He provides when all others fail, for it speaks of the restoration of His joy in life, in service, in the home, in the workplace, for "wine makes glad the heart of man".

We can plan, programme, organize, as they did for the wedding feast, but human endeavour is not sufficient. Christ alone is the source of all true joy; human effort by Christians is subject to failure. Listening is important when the Lord says such things as, "apart from Me you can do nothing" (John 15:5). God wants to fill lives with Christ - that is why it is essential to recognize the significance of the stone water jars being empty at the feast. They remind us that the joy of human effort comes to an end and needs to be replaced with something more enduring. The One who could command light to shine out of darkness, demons to come out of men, multitudes to be fed with a few loaves and fishes, a dead man to come from the grave, that day commanded at Cana: "Fill the waterpots with water". It was done. "Draw out now", He again commanded, "and bear to the ruler of the feast". That was done, and immediately the water changed to wine. One who drank described it as "good wine". Good means worthy, virtuous, valuable, the very adjectives used to describe Christ as the Good Shepherd. So

Cana, the place of reeds, became the place of provision.

The blessings of protection and provision at the place of the reeds can encourage Christians to value more than ever a quiet place beside the still waters, as David did, for restoration of soul. Quiet times with the living word where we can find the joy of Christ seem to be more needful than ever in these days of stress and uncommon demand. We can view our Bible as our stone jar filled with the precious water of life in all its refreshment, and as we draw out and taste we experience that joy, satisfaction, comfort, and peace, which comes with knowing Christ, whom to know is life eternal. He is our protector and provider, One who never fails. Daily we need to hear His quiet whisper as we read and meditate: "Draw out now". And we do so, for our benefit and that of others.

17: JOY RESTORED

I will restore to you the years that the swarming locust has eaten."
(Joel 2:25 NKJV).

Only small in size, but what havoc is wrought by the locust! Only a couple of inches long, but what desolation it leaves in its train! When the locust sets out on its mission its determined purpose is to devour every green blade in its way, and this is accomplished by the steady nibble, nibble, nibble until all grass and plants are eaten. In the prophecy of Joel we construe that God's ancient people must have suffered drastically from the swarms of locusts. Fruit orchards would be stripped, pastureland and grain fields ravaged, and the ultimate result would be famine. Then we see the kindness and mercy of God towards the children of Zion in the divine promise:

"I will restore to you the years that the swarming locust has eaten ... you shall eat in plenty and be satisfied, and praise the Name of the LORD your God, who has dealt wondrously with you." Our God is a great Restorer! He is the Restorer of the soul (Psalm 23); He is the Restorer of the joy of salvation (Psalm 51); and He is the Restorer of the years that the locusts have eaten (Joel 2). Do we need restoring as

God's people today, individually, collectively? What of those days, and months, and years of our spiritual lives which have been nibbled away until the green leaf of our Christian experience has been almost destroyed? An accumulation of small things which are not of God can quickly turn an otherwise fresh, wholesome spiritual life into barren desolation. Is the Lord getting from us what He deserves, and what belongs to Him? Are we able to give Him the invitation of the Bride to her Beloved in the Song of Songs? She said, "Let my Beloved come into His garden, And eat His precious fruits" (4:16).

Or are our lives like some "barren waste with thorns o'ergrown," nothing much left for Him but parched land? It is sometimes hard to realize that such a thing can happen to the child of God. The truth of this was once portrayed in a poem the theme of which was, "Amid an upturned field a rusty plough." Described vividly in verse was the scene of the once prosperous farm, now in a state of obvious neglect, the farmhouse in disrepair, once fruitful fields now overgrown with weeds, and amidst the ruins and neglect a rusty plough in a partly upturned field. What of the owner? What of his heritage, his precious possessions, the fruits of his toil once earned by the sweat of his brow? Nothing to show but barren desolation, and the mute testimony of a rusty plough! How solemn are the Master's words in the light of this! "No man, having put his hand to the plough, and looking back, is fit for the kingdom of God" (Luke 9:62).

How vital is the work of restoration in these lives of ours to rectify those things which we have neglected! Our prayer life, our assembly life, our study of the word, our testimony to the world by deed and word, our care of our Sunday school class, seeking our neighbour's good by visitation, in conversation on bus and train, by mailing or door-to-door distribution of gospel and believers' booklets, visitation to the hospitals, words of comfort to the bereaved - these are only a beginning, but they can be the beginning of a great recovery from barrenness to fruitfulness.

The ensuing joy will be like that of Mephibosheth when he was brought up from Lo-debar ("the place of no pasture"). Crippled, neglected, unworthy, yet there was shown unto him by David the kindness of God, and he was restored to the place of a prince at the king's table. His joy knew no bounds as he looked into the king's face amidst the beautiful surroundings of the palace, and as he remembered the parched wasteland of Lo-debar. May we heed the spiritual lesson in this particular incident!

Some years ago a young Christian woman lay on her deathbed in a sanatorium. She had been saved as a young girl, but growing cold in heart she drifted away from the Saviour's love. Entering womanhood, she contracted tuberculosis, and as she lay dying in hospital she sent for the man who led her to Christ. At the bedside he endeavoured to comfort her by re-telling the story of her salvation, but as he was leaving her she cried to him, "Oh those wasted years!" Thus she died, sad to say, but these words might apply to some of us, today, to us who are blessed with health and strength, and are letting the days slip by and rendering so little service to the One who has done so much for us. May the dying embers of love to our Lord Jesus be rekindled in our souls, the joy of salvation revived, and the year that the locusts have eaten restored!

18: JOY IN PRAISING GOD

"O h that men would praise the LORD for His goodness, and for His wonderful works to the children of men!" (Psalm 107:8). Three times the Psalmist repeats this verse, with the reasons why the Lord should be praised.

There is joy in praising God. The Old Testament saints knew this when they entered into the gates of the Lord with thanksgiving, and into His courts with praise (Psalm 100:4). Though they had not known the love of God in sending His Son as we have, yet they knew His goodness and His wonderful works. The praising life prepares us for the Remembrance of our Lord Jesus Christ each Lord's day. Even if we are few in number, when we are led by the Spirit of God and all say Amen because we are one in heart, then we feel the joy of heaven.

Revelation chapter 5 shows the praise and adoration in heaven. Four living creatures, and twenty four elders fall down before the Lamb, and they sing a new song: "You are worthy art ... for You were slain, and have redeemed us to God by Your blood, out of every tribe, and tongue, and people, and nation" (v.9).

Then a great multitude of angels around the throne and the living creatures and the elders said with a great voice: "Worthy is the Lamb who was slain, to receive power and riches, and wisdom, and strength, and honour, and glory and blessing! (v.12). Then every created thing responded, and "the four living creatures said, "Amen". And the ... elders fell down and worshipped."

When we consider the praise and adoration of these heavenly beings, we realize how far short we come in our thanksgiving and praise to God. Yet it was for us that Jesus died, and through Him our Spirit-led praise reaches to the throne. How sad it is if we have little to give. It is good for us to prepare ourselves for each Lord's day morning. It is good to put away newspapers, and not to use the radio or television for the world's news on the Lord's day. We cannot think freely of the Lord when our minds are stored with earthly things, or even if we are thinking of our own joys and sorrows. We need a quiet mind to worship God.

"O come, let us sing unto the LORD: Let us make a joyful noise to the Rock of our salvation" (Psalm 95:1)

The Remembrance of the Lord Jesus Christ in the broken bread and poured-out wine is a time when "we sing with sweetest sadness" as we consider again the blood-like sweat and the shameful tree. It is right that we should be moved again in our spirits, each Lord's day, as we reverently consider all that He passed through on our account. But it is also a time when we should rejoice in His glorious resurrection, for He is risen. The everlasting doors have been lifted up, and the King of Glory has entered in (Psalm 24:9). We move on in worship from the Cross to the Resurrection for, "He arose, Hallelujah, Christ arose!" Not only so, He presents to the Father the praise and adoration of the saints. Through Him we offer up a sacrifice of praise to God. We remember that, "the Father sent the Son to be the Saviour of the world" (1 John 4:14).

"The streams of love I trace
Up to the fountain, God;
And in His sovereign counsels see
Eternal thoughts of love to me".

And so our "songs of sweetest sadness" become songs of joy and praise as we contemplate the majesty of the Divine Being whom we worship and adore. In a coming day every created thing in the heaven and on the earth, and under the earth, will say, "Blessing and honor and glory and power *be* to Him who sits on the throne, and to the Lamb, forever and ever" (Revelation 5:13). It is to this lofty height we should aspire every Lord's day while together for worship and praise. The Cross made it possible for us to draw near to the Throne.

If our worship does not reach the lofty strains of adoration and praise to Him who sits upon the Throne, and to the Lamb, then we ourselves will feel that we have come short. The Cross and the tomb are hallowed scenes, brought to our remembrance as we partake of the broken bread and poured-out wine, but these are the beginnings of the Spirit's leadings as we show forth the Lord's death until He come. As we go forth from these times of praise and adoration, let us remember that it is but a little while and He will come. Then "in songs of sweet untiring praise, we will to everlasting days, make all His glories known".

19: JOY IN TRIALS

You will remember the lines of the well-known hymn: Have we trials or temptations, Is there trouble anywhere? The answer to the question must quite often be "Yes". We do have trials, even though we have taken the Lord Jesus as Saviour and committed our lives to Him. Trials are those experiences which come to oppress us and the Lord Jesus never promised that our lives as Christians would be all smooth and free from them. Rather the reverse; if we follow Him faithfully there will inevitably be trials in our lives. So, when James writes in his letter about trials, he doesn't say, "If they come", he says "Whenever they come" (1:2) - for come they surely will.

We read in the book of Daniel, chapter 3, of trial of the severest kind that came to three young men who took their stand for God. The decree of the great autocrat had been proclaimed; everyone must bow to the image he had set up. The penalty for refusal was death of the cruellest kind - burning in a superheated furnace. But those men couldn't bow to that image. They were servants of the God of heaven and owed their allegiance to Him. So they were faced with the most searching trial, to yield and live, or to stand firm and die. They stood firm, testifying to the king that their God was able to deliver them from the furnace if that was His will. But if it was not His will then He had the power to enable them to go through the furnace. Their faith was well founded. They were not delivered from the furnace; God's will was that they should go into it, but they had the presence of God with them there and they came out unscathed. God is always in control. He will not suffer us to be tried beyond what we are able but, as 1 Corinthians 10:13 says, "He will also provide a way out so that you can stand up under it".

James in his New Testament letter says a remarkable thing, "Consider it pure joy whenever you face trial". It seems so unlikely, doesn't it, that we could consider facing a trial as pure joy? We could perhaps face it stoically without grumbling too much or having too mournful a face - but to treat it as pure joy, how can we do that? Only as we realize that God has a purpose in trials for us, and His purposes are always for our good. Trials are for our refining. As we come through them with His help they are proof of our faith and they lead to steadfastness.

Then too, we must realize that the Lord will be with us in the trial, keeping close, just as He did with the men in the furnace. He is touched with the feeling of our infirmities and we can seek His aid, approaching the throne of grace with confidence that we may receive mercy and find grace to help us in our time of need.

20: GIDEON

D epressed, discouraged, fearful: these appeared to be Gideon's symptoms when the angel of the Lord addressed him as a "mighty man of valour". Did he deserve such a divine commendation? Yes, because he seemed to be the only one doing something to feed the people of God in a time of great adversity.

The marauding Midianites, with their fleet-footed camels, had completely changed Israel's way of life. Instead of enjoying peace in a land they had conquered, God's people were forced to exist in dens and caves, the habitat of wild animals. They were robbed of their crops, vines, sheep, and cattle. What a contrast to the prosperity and promise associated with the early possession of a land they had effectively subdued!

Although this occurred over 3,000 years ago, there is a message in it for the people of God today. Our warfare is spiritual, our promised land is the heavenly places, and our enemy is Satan and his hosts of wickedness. Are they depriving us of the full joy of what God has made available in Christ's work at Calvary? Instead of being happy, vibrant, prosperous Christians, is it possible that we are living deprived, unhappy, fearful, starved lives, because our enemy has gained the upper hand? Is this possible? Is it true? Moffatt gives this graphic translation of Ephesians 6:12, "For we have to struggle not with blood and flesh but with the angelic Rulers, the angelic Authorities, the potentates of the dark present, the spirit-forces of evil in the heavenly sphere. So take God's armour ..." We cannot afford to be on the losing side as Israel was, early in Gideon's day.

Gideon was beating out wheat in the winepress because he had a shepherd's care for God's sheep. The shallow pit, which was the lower part of the winepress, was where Gideon stood day after day secretly producing food, and distributing it before the enemy swooped down to steal it. The smallness of the winepress contrasted with the wide, open area of the normal threshing-floor; its use for threshing wheat clearly indicates the absence of joy in the land, for the winepress was for the crushing of grapes to produce wine which makes the heart of man glad" (Psalm 104:15). No grapes were being crushed. It was at this time God turned towards Gideon and spoke to him the reassuring words: "Surely I will be with you" (Judges 6:16).

The assurance of divine presence was reinforced by the Lord granting him His peace, and Gideon built an altar, naming it Jehovah-Shalom (v.24). After destroying his father's idol (v.28), Gideon was further strengthened by the Spirit of the Lord coming upon him (y.34). Surely he was now ready for the great task of leading Israel' into victorious battle. Gideon proved to be a brave man in a day of adversity. His example can encourage us in today's spiritual warfare against an ever present enemy in the spiritual realm. Take courage, beloved, "The LORD is with you" (Judges 6:12).

21: JOY THROUGH WALKING, STANDING AND SITTING

salm 1 pronounces blessing in three well-worded triplets. "He is a happy man who walks not in the counsel of the wicked, nor stands in the way of sinners, nor sits in the seat of the scornful. Such a man has his delight in the law of the LORD. In it he meditates day and night." In the root of the Hebrew word for meditation is the imagery of a lion growling for sheer joy over his meat. What a delightful, if somewhat forceful, contemplation of the man or woman of God in the thorough day-to-day enjoyment of the reading and pondering of the Word.

Let us look briefly at these three conditions of spiritual experience that will result in happiness:

(1) Walking with God

The experience is as old as Eden and was first broken there. The LORD God brought to Adam every beast and fowl to see what he would call them. It was the beginnings of God walking with men. And in the cool of the day of Adam's transgression our first parents heard what had formerly been to them the well-loved voice, as the LORD God walked in the garden and called them. But now their walking days with God had ceased, nor would they be resumed till communion was restored.

In due course Enoch came, and he "walked with God ... three hundred years". It was a long walk in a dark day. Jude described many of his contemporaries as "wild waves of the sea, foaming out their own shame; wandering stars, for whom the blackness of darkness hath been reserved for ever". Fearless, Enoch denounced them in the words of the prophecy disclosed centuries later through Jude (verses 13-15). Thus men who habitually walk with God are in a state of communion and in a position to speak for God His message regarding others.

Then Noah came and he too walked with God. On every hand was corruption and violence; already there was "no fear of God before their eyes". But this walker with God was in communion with his God and as a result Noah received the revelation of His purposes for that day. So he became "a preacher of righteousness" to "the world of the ungodly", and his walk of faith found expression in his work of faith.

Then Abram came, and he too walked with God. He had heard the call beyond the River, where "they served other gods". He separated himself and came to the land of God's choice for him. There the men of the cities of the plain "were wicked and sinners against the LORD exceedingly", but Abram maintained his separation, regardless of financial cost. To such a man the LORD appeared, saying, "I am God

Almighty; walk before Me, and be thou perfect". What a demand, what a standard! Yet it developed into what might fittingly be compared to the long walk of a man with his friend, for Abram became known as "the friend of God". So God communed with him (Genesis 18:33) and Abram came into the secrets of His counsel.

Then Levi came and of him (and in particular of Aaron his priestly descendant) Malachi wrote some lovely things, centuries later. "He walked with Me in peace and uprightness, and did turn many from iniquity. For the priest's lips should keep knowledge and they should seek the law at his mouth: for he is the messenger of the LORD of hosts" (Malachi 2:4-7). Thus "Levi", in his walk with God, knew inward peace and showed outward uprightness, and by reason of his communion with the LORD he became His messenger to His people.

And so, down the ages, men and women learned to walk with God. Those of Old Testament days are brilliantly reviewed in Hebrews 11, where, as here, time would fail to name them. But all walking with God reached its glorious climax when the Son of God was here, and men "looked upon Jesus as He walked". That was the supreme walk of unmarred, unbroken communion, from Bethlehem to Calvary, Father and Son going both of them together. Others were privileged from time to time to share in the joy of that walk, perhaps never so choicely expressed as when He drew near to the two on the Emmaus highway. Of that momentous experience they later said, "Was not our heart burning within us, while He spoke to us in the way, while He opened to us the Scriptures?"

So men and women still walk in communion with Him, and their hearts still burn until, "While I was musing the fire kindled: then I spoke with my tongue (Psalm 39:3). Little wonder the Holy Spirit said, "See then that you walk circumspectly, not as fools but as wise, redeeming the time, because the days are evil" (Ephesians 5:15-16 NKJV). So much depends upon it.

> Such be the tribute of thy pilgrim journey
> When life's last mile thy feet have bravely trod
> When thou hast gone to all that there awaits thee,
> This simple epitaph - "He walked with God".
> (J. Danson Smith)

(2) Standing in His presence

When the owner of the vineyard went into the market "about the eleventh hour he went out and found others standing idle and said to them, 'Why have you been standing here idle all day? (Matthew 20:6). Standing idle all the day; hired just in time at the eleventh hour.

Gabriel, the angel, said to Zacharias, "I am Gabriel, that stand in the presence of God; and I was sent ..." (Luke 1:19). Standing and sent. Gabriel was not standing idle. No beings in the divine Presence stand idle. When Ezekiel was privileged to see them, he noted that they "ran and returned as the appearance of a flash of lightning" (Ezekiel 1:14). Winds, and a flame of fire, was how the psalmist described those who stand in His presence (Psalm 104:4).

Elijah said, "As the LORD, the God of Israel lives, before whom I stand (1 Kings 17:1). So when the word of the LORD came to him, saying, Go, he went; whether it was to the court of the wicked Ahab in 1 Kings 17:1, or to the infuriated Ahab in 1 Kings 18:1. Human or angelic, it matters not, those who stand habitually in the presence of God are not only given messages for others but are also instant in their commission. Who among us would not long and pray for this experience of standing in His presence, and being sent forth commissioned?

Of others we read that when they stood in the divine Presence it was in a ministry Godward. Indeed "ministering spirits, sent forth" may well indicate a Godward ministry combined with an outward-bound service. We recall the word of good king Hezekiah to the Levites, "My sons, do not be negligent now, for the LORD has chosen you to stand before Him, to serve Him, and that you should minister to Him and burn incense" (2 Chronicles 29:11). So in the divine Presence some men were honoured to stand in a Godward ministry, some offering incense, some lifting up their hands to the sanctuary blessing God in the service of praise. The latter were employed in this work day and night, the singers being 288 in number, thus enabling the twelve tribes to enjoy a twenty-four hour representation in the Temple worship.

Standing in the presence of God. They stand close who love His Word, reading it, meditating on it, then going out to live it. The wise king described it for God this way, "Blessed is the man that listens to Me, watching daily at My gates, waiting at the posts of My doors" (Proverbs 8:34 NKJV). Hearing, watching, waiting at God's doorpost. No wonder doorkeepers in the LORD'S 'house of old loved their assignment. They were sons of Korah. Other of his sons were chosen to be singers. They went right inside the beautiful building in their service. The doorkeepers only stood at the threshold. But they said, "I would rather be a doorkeeper in the house of my God, than to dwell in the tents of wickedness" (Psalm 84:10).

Only to stand on the threshold
Though I see not the Master's face,
At the gate of His holy palace
To have my name and my place.
From my post I shall never wander

At my watch I shall never sleep,
And my heart shall sing for gladness
At the door I am set to keep.

Individually we, too, can enjoy today the personal experience of standing in His presence, constantly availing ourselves of the cleansing blood for communion. They hear most who stand closest. They receive greater assignments who stand nearest. Collectively too we may enjoy today the experience of standing in the divine Presence in Godward ministry. We refer particularly to the time of the breaking of the bread. It is then, when gathered to keep the Remembrance of the Lord Jesus, that the people of God draw near in holy priesthood service, responding to the invitation of Hebrews 10:22. The boldness to draw near is one of the glories of the New Covenant, the way of the holies has been dedicated to this sublime purpose, for His people there is "a place of access among them that stand by" (Zechariah 3:7), and the Lord Jesus an enabling Great Priest over the house of God. In all the range of God's dealings with His people, was there ever so glorious an era as this, so complete an experience of divine service?

(3) Sitting at His feet

From earliest times the learner sat at the teacher's feet, actually or metaphorically. There was a God-given principle in it, for at Sinai, it was said of Israel "They sit down at Your feet; *Everyone* receives Your words." (Deuteronomy 33:3). They sat to receive and to bear away. Elijah was taken away from the head of Elisha (2 Kings 2:5), so the young man who poured water on his hands also sat at his feet. Then in due course the sons of the prophets sat at the feet of Elisha (2:15).

Paul said at his Jerusalem defence that he had been "brought up in this city, at the feet of Gamaliel, taught ..." (Acts 22:3). He had been reared and nourished there in the spiritual sphere, just as Moses had been in the physical, first in his mother's home and then in the palace of Pharaoh's daughter. And both men emerged as giants in their own sphere.

In the fragrant Bethany home, the two sisters prepared for their much-loved Guest, and at some point Mary left her sister and "also sat at the Lord's feet, and heard His word" (Luke 10:39). Martha, excellent Martha, went alone to serve an elaborate meal to the point of personal distraction. But Mary knew something of the secret of the proper apportionment of time between serving and sitting at His feet. She was criticised for her choice, misunderstood in this and other things, but in sitting awhile at His feet and listening she had chosen "the good part" and would never lose it, nor the things she heard. "And it was that Mary which anointed the Lord with ointment, and wiped His feet with her hair" (John 11:2). To her they were lovely feet, with the beauty of which Isaiah had written in Isaiah 52:7.

As she sat beside them and listened, she saw what others failed to see; she saw impending Calvary and, regardless of cost, brought her very precious spikenard and anointed Him in anticipation of His burial. So far as we know she did not go to the tomb with the others, but He went over against where she lived for His ascension. In her sitting she had understood, and He appreciated it. Taking the time to sit at His feet and listen resulted then and results still in intelligent service, most acceptable to Him. Our heavenly Lover still yearns for those who, in a day of many pressures and advancing knowledge in things which are doomed to pass away, still take time to feel at home amid eternal things, will still find it their delight to sit at His feet, to stand in His presence, to walk at His side.

Only to stand on the threshold,
Ah l this were heaven to me,
After the weary desert,
After the wintry sea.
But I hear Him call me higher
In accents long and sweet
I shall not stand on the threshold
But sit at the Master's feet.

22: THE JOY OF THE BEATITUDES- PART 2

This chapter continues to take a look at the secret of happiness (blessedness) that Jesus revealed to his followers in the Sermon on the Mount.

"Blessed are the meek"

There is a great deal of confusion about the subject of meekness. Many people are not clear exactly what it means. The Bible says the man Moses was very meek, in fact, the meekest man in all the earth. And it makes that comment at the time when his sister and brother spoke against him because of his wife. Their complaint was completely unfounded and it must have been very hard for Moses to bear. But he didn't attempt to justify himself. There was nothing in him which rose in self-defence. He was content to leave it with God. That was meekness. There is certainly no thought of weakness in it. On the contrary, it is evidence of great spiritual strength.

When the Lord Jesus came to live on earth, He said, "I am meek and lowly in heart" (RV). He showed us meekness in perfection. There was no thought of self in Him at all. "When He was reviled, He did not revile in return; when He suffered, He did not threaten; but He trusted to Him who judges justly" (1 Peter 2:23). He must have felt keenly the pain of the scourging and beating, for He was a Man like ourselves. And even more deeply He felt the cruelty and mockery that were hurled at Him. But it produced no resentment in His heart. There was nothing within which rose up in self-defence, or even in self-pity. That was meekness in perfection. And Jesus said, "Blessed are the meek." This is the way to real blessing, to the sort of happiness which God loves to give.

But the reward of the meek is "they shall inherit the earth." How and when we ask? I suppose there's a sense in which they inherit it now, if you take the apostle Paul as an example. "I have all things, and abound" he says (Philippians 4:18 RV). "There is great gain in godliness with contentment" (1 Timothy 6:6). There's no doubt about that, and those who have learned that secret would not wish to change places with anyone else.

But I think the Lord Jesus was speaking primarily of a future day when lie comes to reign, and those who have taken their part in suffering with Him now will reign with Him then. "Do you not know that the saints will judge the world?" asked the apostle Paul of the Corinthians (1 Corinthians 6:2). They ought to have known, but from the way they were behaving I think they had forgotten. Let us not forget. But let Christ's word come right into our hearts today. "Blessed are the meek, for they shall inherit the earth."

The Jewish leaders of Christ's day were expecting Him to seize the reins of government and set up His kingdom and reign as king. But it didn't work that way. He was coming to reign, but not then. The way to the throne was via the cross. Meek and lowly and riding upon an ass, He came into the capital city to die. And He asks us to follow where He has led the way. The world around us thinks so differently. They think in terms of strength and aggressiveness. That's the world's idea of conquest. But the Man of Calvary, meek and lowly in heart, is still calling us His way, the way of real happiness. "Blessed are the meek, for they shall inherit the earth."

"Blessed are those who hunger and thirst"

Consider the next blessing the Lord Jesus pronounced in His Sermon on the Mount. "Blessed are those who hunger and thirst for righteousness, for they shall be satisfied." Notice it is not those who hunger and thirst for happiness there are plenty of people like that, and they're never satisfied. But those who hunger and thirst for righteousness, these are the ones who are satisfied, and that satisfaction brings real happiness. The Lord Jesus said so, and many people the world over are proving His words true.

God speaks about righteousness in two different ways. There is the righteousness which is ours in Christ. It belongs to all who are born again. You remember the apostle Paul says at the end of 2 Corinthians 5, "For our sake He (that is God) made Him (the Lord Jesus) to be sin who knew no sin, so that in Him we might become the righteousness of God." In that sense God sees all who believe as righteous in Christ. Then there is the righteousness we show in our actions because we are born again. "If you know that He is righteous, you may be sure that every one who does right is born of Him" the apostle John says (1 John 2:29). The first has to do with our justification. God counts us righteous in Christ. The second affects our sanctification which here is a daily experience. "Yield your members to righteousness for sanctification," says Paul in Romans 6:19. In other words we use our bodies to live holy lives.

Righteousness! That is God's standard of what is right. The world cares nothing about it, and the world is not a happy place. Moral standards are crumbling all around us. Men have set aside God's standards but with disastrous results in family life, and with an alarming increase in violence and robbery. Many thoughtful people are wondering what sort of a world our children are being born into. If only men and nations would heed the words of the Lord Jesus they would find the happiness and contentment they are so desperately seeking. "Blessed are those who hunger and thirst for righteousness, for they shall be satisfied." These are the happy people.

I'll never forget one of our Chinese friends who lived in Rangoon in Burma. His conversion was very real to him and he just fell in love with the Lord and with his Bible. He was like the blessed man of Psalm 1 who meditated in God's law night and day. No wonder he made such rapid progress spiritually. Everything he read in his Bible he related to his own life. As far as he was concerned all God's commandments were to be obeyed. He almost literally hungered and thirsted after righteousness, and you couldn't have wished for a happier or more contented man.

It's an interesting expression the Lord Jesus uses, for a hungry man just grows more hungry and a thirsty man more thirsty until he is satisfied. And then appetite repeats the process all over again, for hunger and thirst return, and increase, until once again they're satisfied. "As a hart longs for flowing streams, so longs my soul for Thee, O God. My soul thirsts for God, for the living God." "But that's not my experience," you may say. "I don't have that sort of longing after God. I only wish I had." Ah! Christian, it will come, if you get to your Bible. Spend time on your knees each day, asking God to speak to you out of His Word, and you will find your appetite beginning to grow. The more you read and meditate, the more you'll enjoy it, until you are hungering and thirsting for more. The only condition is that you obey what God says, for that is where the righteousness comes in. And then you will understand what Job meant when he said, "I have treasured up the words of His mouth more than my necessary food" (Job 23:12 RV).

"Blessed are the merciful"

One of the highlights of our service for the Lord in Burma was a weekly visit to the local jail. The authorities gave us permission to have a Bible reading with as many of the men as wished to come, and great times they were. The message was so new to most of them. You could see the surprise registering on their faces as the story unfolded. That there was a God in heaven who loved them despite their sin was something wonderful. And to lift them out of it and give them power over it, sending His Son to die, was more wonderful still. Week after week God gave power to His Word, and we marvelled to see it going deep into the hearts of these rough men. In some it worked conviction of sin, and turned them to Christ for salvation.

One of the first to be saved was a college graduate, in for murder. He was naturally quick-tempered and had given the warders a hard time. So when he came to Christ everybody saw the change. Standing up one day in front of the other men he gave his testimony, and we saw the tears trickling down the faces of some of those hardened criminals. "I thought there was no hope for me," he said, "but when I heard of God's love in sending His Son, it dawned on me there was mercy even for me!" How true! There is no limit to His mercy. "God who is rich in mercy, out of the great love with which He loved us, even when we were dead through our trespasses, made us alive with Christ." It has been said that God's grace reaches men in their sin, and His mercy reaches them in their misery. It is God's pity in action, reaching down for our help. "When the kindness of God our Saviour, and His love toward man appeared ... according to His mercy He saved us" (Titus 3:4-5 RV).

Has the mercy of God reached you? If so, then God expects you to show mercy to others. "Blessed are the merciful, for they shall obtain mercy" the Lord Jesus said. The good Samaritan showed it the day he met the man dying by the roadside. The priest and the Levite passed by on the other side. But the Samaritan concerned himself with his fellow-traveller's need, and did all in his power to help him. When he had brought him safely to the inn and made provision for him to be well cared for, he went on his way with a glad heart. How do I know that? Because the Lord Jesus said, "Blessed are the merciful." There's no happiness to be compared with this. The world seeks its happiness by getting. The Lord Jesus said it comes by giving.

He told of the servant who owed his master ten thousand talents and because he could not pay his master had mercy on him and forgave him the whole debt. And then he went out and laid hands on one of his fellow-servants who owed him a trivial amount in comparison, and threw him into prison until he paid up. His master was very angry and said "I forgave you all that debt because you besought me; and should not you have had mercy on your fellow-servant, as I had mercy on you?" (Matthew 18:32-33).

Of course he should! And the Lord Jesus added this solemn lesson for us all, that we must forgive one another from the heart. Notice that. It must be a heart matter. Not just from our lips but genuinely from our hearts. For if we don't there is the solemn possibility that we shall not be forgiven either. May the Lord's message go deep into our hearts: "Blessed (happy) are the merciful, for they shall obtain mercy."

23: LOST AND FOUND JOY

S omeone or something found can provide a great deal of delight and satisfaction. Examples are seen in a person, a sheep, or money, and even the mould on a petri dish in a laboratory which led to the discovery of penicillin.

But what of those spiritual realities which when found have provided great joy for men and women. The moving words of dear humble Ruth, for example, as she bows herself before Boaz, saying, "Why have I found grace in your sight ... seeing that I am a stranger?" (Ruth 2:10). Amidst the idolatry of Moab Ruth responds to the good news of Israel's loving God and His elect people with this confession, "... your people shall be my people, and your God my God" (Ruth 1:16). Brought to her new home, she is overwhelmed by the loving care and interest of Boaz her future husband, who brings her into the royal line of Israel. What tremendous blessings were brought to Ruth by grace, and to us too. But have we Ruth's spirit of appreciation, or has ours waned? If we have been saved by grace, made living stones in God's house, brought into the holy priesthood and the holy nation, we might well ask: Why? Our answer should be in a gracious heart response for we are unworthy of the least of God's mercies.

Job is jubilant in the personal knowledge of his living Redeemer whom his eyes will behold (19:25,27); but his comforter Elihu, rejoices in God's purpose in opening a man's ears (33:16), delivering him from going down into the pit, so that he might cry: "I have found a ransom" (33:24). What a discovery this is to have found atonement (AV Margin) in One who is able and willing to cover, cleanse, cancel sins and bring about reconciliation, complete pardon. What rejoicing should fill the heart as we exclaim: Thank You, Lord for saving my soul; Thank You, Lord for making me whole. But do we show our jubilation? "And let Your saints shout for joy", says David (Psalm 132:9).

The consort of the beloved in the Song of Songs has lost him. She grieves, is anxious, and determinedly she seeks him, looking and enquiring for him, until the joyous moment - "I found him ... I held him, and would not let him go" (3:14). What a contrast to the disappointment of, "I sought him, but found him not" (v.2). Here is an example of communion, happiness, restored. It is so easy for the Christian to know loss of fellowship with the Beloved in these days of demands on our time and lives. We must recognize that things can so easily replace the Lord Jesus in our lives. "There is so much to do: I cannot keep pace as it is; the pressures are heavier; the stress is getting to me", are familiar descriptions of those things which cause us to lose the sense of His presence. We forget at times that it is His presence which enables us to cope with the demands of home, work, and church responsibilities. Without Him we can gradually sink under burdens and flounder in despair. The answer: Find Him - the One whom your soul loves! Give Him the place He deserves in your affection.

Hold Him joyously, thankfully, and do not let Him go again.

Solomon sought wisdom, knowledge, mirth, pleasure, wine, great works, houses, vineyards, gardens, silver, gold, peculiar treasure, but in the end he had to admit, "I looked on all the works that my hands had wrought ... all was vanity and a striving after wind ... So I hated life" (Ecclesiastes 1:16; 2:1-17). He sought, but found not. Sufficient for it to be said of us, "We have found Him ... Jesus" (John 1:45).

24: JOY THROUGH REMEMBERING

Today's busy, demanding life can rob Christians of their "Selah" joy: that joy which comes from pausing to consider the love of Christ. There seems to be so little time to pause and consider; and, incidentally, to remember. The Greek word translated "to remember" infers exercising or punishing the mind. Effort on our part is involved. In the Hebrew, earnestness is indicated. For us, then, to remember is serious business.

God remembers, and He first uses the word in Scripture in relation to Noah, the flood, and the rainbow: "That I may remember the everlasting covenant" (Genesis 9:16). Pharaoh's butler set an example for us to follow: "I do remember my faults this day" (Genesis 41:9). Hundreds of years later Moses counselled Israel to remember their day of deliverance from Egypt's bondage (Exodus 13:3). Annually this was celebrated in the Passover. Covenants were to be remembered, the blessings of the Lord, and memories of the patriarchs. Three times Nehemiah asks the Lord to remember him (13:31); the psalmist pleads, "Remember how short my time is" (89:47). "Remember also your

Creator in the days of your youth", pleads Solomon (Ecclesiastes 12:1); "Remember this, and show yourselves men", said Isaiah to Israel's idol worshipping remnant as he reminded them of God's faithfulness from birth to old age (Isaiah 46:8); Israel's blindness and love are remembered by the Lord (Jeremiah 2:2), and we see His grace, in that He would no more remember their sin (31:34); and Habakkuk pleads "in wrath remember mercy" (Habakkuk 3:2).

When His disciples moaned about forgetting bread for their journey, the Lord Jesus chided them that they did not "remember the five loaves of the five thousand and how many baskets you took up (Matthew 16:9)? "Remember Lot's wife", was another of His wise warnings (Luke 17:32). Yet, one thing that should cause us to rejoice, was the Lord's response to the dying thief who cried: "Jesus, remember me when You come into Your kingdom". Instantly He responded with words of grace and assurance, "Today, you will be with Me in Paradise" (Luke 23:42). Such love, such willingness to forgive even at the eleventh hour! Such grace should be remembered by us. And what shall we say of the angels' reminder to the perplexed but faithful women who found an empty tomb? "Remember how He spoke to you... that the Son of man must be delivered into the hands of sinful men, and be crucified and the third day rise again. And they remembered His words" (Luke 24:1-8).

In review, perhaps our meditation will bring to our remembrance the spiritual value and blessing of the New Covenant; of the confession and forgiveness of our sins; of our deliverance from bondage; of Christ being our Passover; of God's faithfulness; His innumerable blessings through Christ, and our weekly remembrance of Him with the bread and wine. This is a blessed occasion when we are welcomed into God's presence as a holy priesthood to remember, to worship, to praise, to give thanks: an honour we must always remember and value.

Lest I forget Gethsemane,
Lest I forget Thine agony,
Lest I forget Thy love for me,
Lead me to Calvary".

25: GETTING CLOSER TO JOY

The inner spark has gone and you know there is something wrong. Tiredness has taken over; instead of being lively you are a lethargic Christian. Reality is missing and you find yourself functioning like a robot, doing things in a lifeless, automatic way. Being on the "fast track" of life has taken away your time for prayer, Bible reading, and the quiet time. Having "too much on my plate", we conclude, is the cause of the tiredness, the "headachy" symptoms, and the reason for the vanishing appetite for spiritual things. And, the Lord is not as near, not as evident as he used to be.

This analysis is not imaginary; it reflects what is happening in the lives of many Christians today. It represents a confession, a cry for help on their part. The need is desperate in some cases, and a helpful solution is essential. Perhaps the story of a native Indian boy can provide part of an answer. His father had taught him much of tribal lore and customs, and once took him on a trek miles from home. Before night fell they enjoyed a meal around a bright fire after a good day together. Then came the great ordeal of the boy spending a night alone in the forest. The father left and the lad adjusted himself to the nightly sights and sounds. On such occasions "the night has a thousand eyes"; plus the cry of the coyote, the wolf, the crash of a running bear, and the rustle of small creatures. It must have been a lonely, sometimes frightening vigil until the dawn began to break, and with it renewed courage and hope. Looking out and around the boy saw a shape which became clearer and clearer. It was his father in the place where he had remained all night. In the darkness, amidst all the sounds and fears, his father had been there all the time. If only he had known!

God had not moved either. He is always there. Whatever our circumstances: trouble, coldness, fear, discouragement, our Father is there - "not far from each one of us" (Acts 17:27). We can talk to Him, tell Him our story, confess our failure, and know His immediate forgiveness to enable us to make a fresh start. "God comes in whenever He is let in".

Probably during the most critical time of his life David cried to God: "Restore to me the joy of Your salvation" (Psalm 51:12). "Restore" is from the Hebrew word shoob, and shepherds are familiar with its meaning: to bring back home, or recover. It is also used in the return of something valuable, such as money, a job, or possessions. Is this what David had in mind when he wrote: "He restores my soul" (Psalm 23:3)? The joy of his salvation and his soul were of supreme importance to David, just as they are to you and me. Perhaps we need to do as Hannah did during her crisis: "I poured out my soul before the LORD" (1 Samuel 1:15). Later she recorded part of the Lord's answer: "He raises the poor from the dust and lifts the beggar from the ash heap, to set them among princes and make them inherit the throne of glory. For the pillars of the earth are the LORD's, and He has set the world upon them. He will guard the feet of His saints ... (1

Samuel 2:8,9).

David cried to the Lord and was heard. Hannah did, too. In like circumstances should we not do the same? We can claim His promises. "From where does my help come?" asks the psalmist. "My help comes from the LORD, who made heaven and earth" (Psalm 121:2) is the answer. In the same portion we are assured: "The LORD is your keeper ... the LORD shall preserve you from all evil; He shall preserve your soul ... your going out and coming in, from this time forth and even for evermore" (vv. 5-8).

To enjoy these things we need to get closer to Him. If He is not far from us we do not have far to move. The thing is to do it.

26: REJOICING IN TRIBULATION

This extract was taken from a book by A.T. Schofield in 1915 and published in NT 50 years later. Fifty years further on and it is as relevant now as it was a century ago!

"… we also glory in tribulations, knowing that tribulation produces perseverance; and perseverance, character; and character, hope …" (Romans 5:3)

True Christians, it seems to me, are of three qualities, which are revealed by the different ways in which tribulations are borne.

The first seem to be made of lead: they murmur and repine and find fault with God in trial, even if they do not lose their trust in Him altogether.

The second are as silver: in tribulation they may show patience and resignation, giving no utterance to impatient or rebellious thoughts though often sorely tried, and tempted to do so.

The third come forth as gold: they rejoice so truly and unaffectedly in their tribulation that friends who come to pity stay to learn their secret.

I have seen those golden ones in trial; and all I can say as a matter of sober personal experience is that they represent, wholly unconsciously, the sublime in suffering. One or two things strike me about them. There is a marked absence of current pious expressions common to some Christians. There is a naturalness and a simplicity and a clearly unaffected and unforced joyfulness that to an ordinary man would certainly seem out of place. You go to see them as sufferers, as I have said, prepared to condole with them, to exhort them to a perfect trust, and to try to cheer them; and before you have been with them five minutes you are dumb, and know not what to say, and hardly what to think, for you are certainly face to face with a miracle. You see before you the finger of God; with them you are consciously in His presence, and you discern in these sufferers a faith that removes mountains, and calls things that are not as though they were. Your little words of sympathy die on your lips in the presence of the great joy before you.

It is marvellous, but so simple! Just as a tiny carbon filament, smaller than a hair, can flood a room with incandescent light when in touch with the storage battery, so does the feeblest and least-taught Christian, when in touch with God, illumine all around.

27: JOY IN THE BEATITUDES - PART 3

The penultimate chapter of the book concludes our look at joy with a look at the final words of Jesus about happiness in his Sermon on the Mount.

"Blessed are the pure in heart"
Have you noticed a progression in the order in which the Lord Jesus spoke the beatitudes? Starting with poverty of spirit, a sense of one's own unworthiness, He went on to pronounce a blessing on those who mourn over sin; and thirdly on the meek, those who have no confidence in self. A meek person recognizes self for what it is, that by his own effort he cannot please God. The first three beatitudes highlight our need and then follows the great statement of that need being met, "Blessed are those who hunger and thirst for righteousness, for they shall be satisfied." Only God can meet the deep need of the human heart, and He meets it absolutely, satisfying us completely. And when the heart is satisfied - flowing out of the blessedness which Christ gives - we become merciful to others, pure in heart, and peace-makers.

Dr. Martyn Lloyd-Jones makes the interesting point that the first three beatitudes correspond to the last three and he links them together in three couplets. The merciful are those who realize their own poverty of spirit, they acknowledge they are nothing in themselves, and that helps them to be merciful to others. And those who are pure in heart have first of all mourned over sin. And the peace-makers are those who are meek in spirit. A person who is not meek is not likely to be very successful in making peace in another person's life.

But think with me, please, about the sixth statement of the Lord Jesus, "Blessed are the pure in heart, for they shall see God." We're all going to see Him, of course, everyone of us who has believed. That is the great prospect the apostle John holds out to us in his first epistle. "Beloved, we are God's children now," he says, "it does not yet appear what we shall be, but we know that when He appears we shall be like Him, for we shall see Him as He is" (3:2). There's a wonderful future ahead of us, Christian. We're going to see our Lord Jesus and be like Him. His servants will do Him service and they will see His face (Revelation 22:3-4).

And then John adds, "Everyone who thus hopes in Him purifies himself as He is pure." If the prospect of being like Him then grips our hearts - if this hope is really working in us - we shall want to be like him now.

Like Him in all those lovely traits,
Which in His lowly, earthly days,
So beautiful we see.

That's what the Lord Jesus was speaking about. "Blessed are the pure in heart, for they shall see God." He himself was absolutely pure and undefiled, and as we keep company with Him we shall grow like

Him. This is one of the great reasons why the Holy Spirit has come to indwell our hearts. He has come to make us like Christ. We're changed into His likeness, Paul says, from one degree of glory to another, for this comes from the Lord who is the Spirit.

And as it takes place, God becomes more real to us, and His fellowship more precious. "Strive for ... holiness" says Hebrews chapter 12, "without which no one will see the Lord" (v.14). That's seeing Him now. We don't have to wait until we get to heaven. Oh no, if we purify ourselves as He is pure, God will become very real to us now. We will live our lives in the light of His presence, and there is no joy to compare with that. If you turn to the first chapter of John's first epistle you will find that's the very thing he is emphasizing. "Our fellowship is with the Father and with His Son Jesus Christ. And we are writing this that your joy may be complete" (RSV Margin). May the Lord lead us all into this completeness of joy. But let us remember it's only possible as we walk in the light. We must resolve we'll set our hearts on, and fill our minds with, whatever is true and honourable and just and pure and lovely and of good report, and then we shall prove His words true, "Blessed are the pure in heart, for they shall see God."

"Blessed are the peacemakers"

We come now to the seventh of the blessings the Lord Jesus pronounced in His Sermon on the Mount, "Blessed are the peacemakers, for they shall be called sons of God."

We live in a world that is desperately seeking peace. But we hear more about war and unrest than we do about peace. Men have done their best to bring peace among the nations many of them honest and sincere men but still it eludes them. Tension grows and nations prepare for war. Why? Why are peace-loving men so unable to establish peace? Because the problem is not political or social, it is rooted deep in the human heart - the problem of sin, for men's hearts are full of lust and greed and selfishness. "There is no peace, says my God, for the wicked." God said that hundreds of years ago through His prophet Isaiah (57:21), and He said it twice over so that men would pay particular attention. And it is as true today as when Isaiah first spoke it. There can be no peace where there is sin.

But God is the great Peacemaker. He is the God of peace. That is one of His lovely titles. And to make peace He sent His Son. "Glory to God in the highest, and on earth peace among men" the angels said as they proclaimed His birth. But His birth alone could not bring peace, nor even His perfect life. Sin had to be dealt with before peace could come. So the Prince of peace went on His lonely way to Calvary, and there He made peace through the blood of His cross. "He was wounded for our transgressions, He was bruised for our iniquities: the chastisement of our peace was upon Him" (Isaiah 53:5 RV). Oh, how we love Him! He made peace. And then He preached peace, to those who were far off, to the many of us who are Gentiles, and to those who were near, our Jewish friends, and through Him we both have our access in one Spirit to the Father.

And now He calls us to the same great work in which He and His Father have been engaged. "Blessed are the peacemakers, for they shall be called sons of God." What a contemplation! You and I can become like God, for that is what it means to be called sons of God as we're engaged in the same glorious work of bringing peace into other people's lives. Being justified by faith we have peace with God ourselves, and now we long that others should find the same peace, first with God and then with their fellows.

Christian, are you a peacemaker? Are you introducing others to the Saviour who died to make their peace with God? And then among your Christian friends are you looking for opportunities of making peace?

"Blessed are those who are persecuted"

We have noticed that the Lord's blessing is promised not on anything we do, but on what we are. It is Christian character that is highlighted in the beatitudes. And we have seen also that the things He values are just the opposite of what the world values. For instance, what time have men in the world got for those who are poor in spirit? "Believe in yourself; push yourself forward;" that's what people say today. But the Lord Jesus teaches us differently. When the Holy Spirit works in our hearts and produces these characteristics, He makes us like Christ. And that immediately makes us different from other people who don't know Him.

The Christian is different. We have to recognize that. And because we are different we may well meet with ridicule and opposition. I'm sure that's why the Lord Jesus added an eighth blessing, for He went on to say, "Blessed are those who are persecuted for righteousness' sake, for theirs is the kingdom of heaven."

Notice, it is those who are persecuted for righteousness' sake. We might be persecuted for other reasons; because of our unwise behaviour, for instance, or even because we hold strong views on certain points. But the Lord Jesus said, "Blessed are you when men revile you and persecute you and utter all kinds of evil against you falsely on my account" or "for My sake." It is when we suffer for His sake he promises the blessing.

Many of our Christian brothers and sisters are suffering for His sake today. Many live in lands where they are denied the freedom to worship and serve the Lord as the Bible teaches. And they are suffering simply because they love the Lord Jesus and they are not afraid to say so. We remember the Lord Jesus said, "If the world hates you, know that it has hated Me before it hated you. If you were of the world, the world would love its own; but because you are not of the world, but I chose you out of the world, therefore the world hates you ... If they persecuted Me, they will persecute you" (John 15:18-20).

And we shall find that is true, in measure at any rate, in whatever land we live. "Indeed all who desire to live a godly life in Christ Jesus will be persecuted" wrote the apostle Paul to Timothy (2 Timothy 3:12). So take courage, Christian!

28: GREAT QUOTES ABOUT JOY

"Joy is the flag you fly when the Prince of Peace is in residence within your heart." Wilfred Peterson

"Joy is not the absence of suffering. It is the presence of God." Robert Schuller

"Joy does not simply happen to us. We have to choose joy and keep choosing it every day." Henri Nouwen

"Joy is the serious business of Heaven." C.S. Lewis

"The only lasting and fully satisfying joys for any man lie on the other side of a cross." Walter J. Chantry

"If you have no joy, there's a leak in your Christianity somewhere." Billy Sunday

"Joy is distinctly a Christian word and a Christian thing. It is the reverse of happiness. Happiness is the result of what happens of an agreeable sort. Joy has its springs deep down inside. And that spring never runs dry, no matter what happens. Only Jesus gives that joy. He had joy, singing its music within, even under the shadow of the cross." S.D. Gordon

"No one can get Joy by merely asking for it. It is one of the ripest fruits of the Christian life, and, like all fruits, must be grown." Henry Drummond

"The essence of loving living as a follower of Jesus isn't in trying harder but in enjoying more. I'm not saying you can change without trying. I'm saying that enjoyment empowers effort. Pleasure in God is the power for purity." Sam Storms

"If we are saved by grace alone, this salvation is a constant source of amazed delight. Nothing is mundane or matter-of-fact about our lives. It is a miracle we are Christians, and the Gospel, which creates bold humility, should give us a far deeper sense of humor and joy. We don't take ourselves seriously, and we are full of hope for the world." Tim Keller

"It is the consciousness of the threefold joy of the Lord, His joy in ransoming us, His joy in dwelling within us as our Saviour and Power for fruitbearing and His joy in possessing us, as His Bride and His delight; it is the consciousness of this joy which is our real strength. Our joy in Him may be a fluctuating thing: His joy in us knows no change." Hudson Taylor

"How sweet all at once it was for me to be rid of those fruitless joys which I had once feared to lose! You drove them from me, You who are the true, the sovereign joy. You drove them from me and took their place, You who are sweeter than all pleasure." Augustine

"You may be lonely, poor, and cold, neglected by the children, forgotten by your friends, yet may have the glad Christmas joy in your heart as Paul had, shut up in prison cells at Rome!" John R. Rice

"I call the New Testament the Book of Joy. There is nowhere in the world another book that is pervaded with such a spirit of exhilaration." Henry Ward Beecher

"The joys of heaven are not the joys of passive contemplation, of dreamy remembrance, of perfect repose; but they are described thus: "They rest not day nor night." His servants serve Him, and see His face." Alexander Maclaren

"Joy has nothing to do with material things, or with a man's outward circumstance ... a man living in the lap of luxury can be wretched, and a man in the depths of poverty can overflow with joy." William Barclay "The angels of heaven rejoice over sinners that repent: saints of God, will not you and I do the same? I do not think the church rejoices enough. We all grumble enough and groan enough: but very few of us rejoice enough. When we take a large number into the church it is spoken of as a great mercy; but is the greatness of that mercy appreciated?" Charles Spurgeon

"The mere fact itself that God's will is irresistible and irreversible fills me with fear, but once I realize that God wills only that which is good, my heart is made to rejoice." A.W. Pink

"I sometimes wonder whether all pleasures are not substitutes for joy." C.S. Lewis

"You must submit to supreme suffering in order to discover the completion of joy." John Calvin

"When the heart is full of joy, it always allows its joy to escape. It is like the fountain in the marketplace; whenever it is full it runs away in streams, and so soon as it ceases to overflow, you may be quite sure that it has ceased to be full. The only full heart is the overflowing heart." Charles Spurgeon

"Oh, what great happiness and bliss, what exaltation it is to address oneself to the Eternal Father. Always, without fail, value this joy which has been accorded to you by God's infinite grace." John of Kronstadt "There is no joy in the world like the joy of bringing one soul to Christ." William Barclay

"Hope fills the afflicted soul with such inward joy and consolation, that it can laugh while tears are in the eye, sigh and sing all in a breath; it is called "The rejoicing of hope." William Gurnall

"There is no virtue in the Christian life which is not made radiant with joy; there is no circumstance and no occasion which is not illuminated with joy. A joyless life is not a Christian life, for joy is one constant recipe for Christian living." William Barclay

"Holy joy will be oil to the wheels of our obedience." Matthew Henry

MORE TITLES FROM HAYES PRESS

If you've enjoyed reading this book, first of all please consider taking a moment to leave a positive review on Amazon! As a thank-you for reading this book, please help yourself to a free download of "Healthy Churches – God's Bible Blueprint For Growth" by Brian Johnston in the Search For Truth Series:

Amazon.com: http://amzn.to/1FuoN5l
Amazon.co.uk: http://amzn.to/1HTSize

Secondly, you may be interested to know that, at the date of the publishing of this book, the Hayes Press catalogue now stands at close to 100 titles; each contains excellent reading material covering a wide range of topics from Bible character studies, theme studies, book studies, apologetics, prophecy, Christian living and more. Ebooks can be purchased on Amazon by searching for Hayes Press. Paperback editions of certain titles are available direct from **www.hayespress.org**

PAPERBACK EDITIONS

The Supremacy of Christ
Once Saved, Always Saved?
Jesus: What Does The Bible Really Say?
The Tabernacle: God's House of Shadows
A Legacy of Kings: Israel's Chequered History
Healthy Churches: God's Bible Blueprint For Growth
Hope For Humanity: God's Fix For A Broken World
Fencepost Turtles: People Placed By God
Minor Prophets – Major Issues
Tribes and Tribulations – Israel's Predicted Personalities
One People For God Omnibus
Kings, Tribes and Prophets Omnibus
God – His Glory, His Building, His Son Omnibus

All these titles are also available in Kindle e-book format from Amazon.

EBOOK EDITIONS

Search For Truth Series
- Overcoming Objections To Christian Faith
- Edge Of Eternity – Approaching The End Of Life
- Tomorrow's Headlines – Bible Prophecy
- An Unchanging God?
- Double Vision – The Insights Of Isaiah
- Abraham – Friend Of God
- Praying With Paul
- Unlocking Hebrews
- They Met At The Cross – Five Encounters With Jesus
- James – The Epistle Of Straw
- The Kingdom of God – Past, Present or Future?
- God's Appointment Calendar: The Feasts of Jehovah
- Seeds – A Potted Bible History

- AWOL! Bible Deserters and Defectors
- 5 Sacred Solos – The Truths That The Reformation Recovered
- Salt & The Sacrifice of Christ
- Turning The World Upside Down
- Windows To Faith
- The Visions of Zechariah
- The Last Words of Jesus
- Closer Than A Brother – Christian Friendship
- Experiencing God in Ephesians
- About The Bush – The Life of Moses
- Trees of the Bible
- After God's Own Heart: The Life of David
- Knowing God: Reflections on Psalm 23
- No Compromise!
- The Glory of God
- Jesus: Son Over God's House
- The Way: New Testament Discipleship
- Esther: A Date With Destiny
- Power Outage: Christianity Unplugged
- Life, the Universe and Ultimate Answers
- Living in God's House
- Answers To Listeners' Questions

Hayes Press Series
- Opened Secrets – Nine Great Bible Mysteries
- The Finger of Prophecy
- Bible Covenants 101
- The Holy Spirit 101
- Satan and His Kingdom
- Profiles of the Prophets: God's Bible Messengers
- Musings on the Minor Prophets
- Discipleship 101 – Basics For Believers
- Ezekiel 101 – Getting To Know God

- What Have We To Give? Bible Devotions From a Missionary
- The Resurrected Christ
- Drawing Near: Prayer In The Old Testament
- Contending For The Faith
- Keys To Church Growth
- Hearts For God: Bible Spiritual Revivals
- Possessing The Land: Spiritual Lessons From Joshua
- God Meant It For Good: The Life Of Joseph
- Moses: God's Deliverer
- Highlights From Hebrews
- The Eternal God Revealed
- In The Shadow Of Calvary: A Bible Study of John 17
- Sparkling Facets – The Names And Titles Of Jesus
- Light From Darke – Seventy Illuminating Devotions
- The Hidden Christ – Types And Shadows In Genesis
- The Return Of Christ
- Exploring Issues Of Life
- Back To Basics
- The Call Of Christ